HARVESTING AND THRESHING

Some tools for agriculture

Introduced by Ian Johnson

Practical
ACTION
PUBLISHING

Intermediate Technology Publications 1987

Practical Action Publishing Ltd
27a Albert Street, Rugby, CV21 2SG, Warwickshire, UK
www.practicalactionpublishing.org

© Intermediate Technology Publications 1987

First published 1987
Digitised 2013
Printed on Demand

ISBN 10: 9 46688 78 8
ISBN 13: 9780946688784
ISBN Library Ebook: 9781780442327
Book DOI: http://dx.doi.org/10.3362/9781780442327

Since 1974, Practical Action Publishing has published and disseminated books and information
in support of international development work throughout the world. Practical Action Publishing
is a trading name of Practical Action Publishing Ltd (Company Reg. No. 1159018), the wholly
owned publishing company of Practical Action. Practical Action Publishing trades only in
support of its parent charity objectives and any profits are covenanted back to Practical Action
(Charity Reg. No. 247257, Group VAT Registration No. 880 9924 76).

Contents

Note: For the full adresses of firms listed in the tables on page 12, see page 28.

HOW TO USE THIS GUIDE

This is one of the twelve sections of the latest edition of *Tools for Agriculture*. Each section is introduced by a specialist who sets the range of tools, implements and machinery available against the background of good farming practice, and the factors best considered when making a choice.

It is intended the guide should be used by the following categories of people:

● Farmers' representatives who purchase equipment on behalf of their clients;
● Advisers who seek to assist farmers and farmers' organizations with the purchase of equipment;
● Development Agency personnel who need to purchase equipment on behalf of farmers and farmers' organizations;
● Prospective manufacturers or manufacturers' agents who wish to have information on the range of equipment currently available.
● Development workers, students and others who wish to learn about the types of equipment available.

We expect the reader to use the guide in one of the following ways:

● to find the name and address of the manufacturer of a specific piece of equipment whose generic name is known e.g. a treadle-operated rice thresher or an animal-drawn turnwrest plough.
● to find the name and address of the manufacturer of a piece of equipment whose general purpose is known e.g. a machine for threshing rice or soil tillage equipment.
● to find out about specific types of equipment or equipment used for specific purposes.
● to find out about the range of equipment available from specific manufacturers or manufacturers in particular countries.
● to learn more about equipment used for the different aspects of crop and livestock production and processing.

Guidance across the broad range of small-scale farming equipment is available, with indexes and cross references, in the parent volume.

Within each section the information is presented in three ways:

● A clear *introduction* which lays out the most important points to bear in mind when purchasing a particular type of equipment. (The emphases vary from section to section — showing the difficulty of decision-making when selecting equipment for smallholder agriculture.)
● *Comprehensive Tables* which list the manufacturers of certain types of equipment and give some further information about specific items, or the range of items manufactured. In many tables it was impossible to give the full address of the manufacturer and the reader is referred for these to the Manufacturer's Index.
● Pages laid out in grid pattern in which the compiler has attempted to present the equipment in a logical order, that in which operations are carried out, and within each type of operation the progress is from hand-operated, through animal-drawn, to motorized equipment. Sometimes one particular type of equipment is illustrated to represent a group — many of which may differ in detail, though not in use. Wherever possible the trade name of the equipment is used, in order to facilitate enquiries to the manufacturers.

Having located a manufacturer for the type of equipment in which you are interested, we suggest you write direct to the manufacturer for further details: current prices, availability, delivery times and so on. (Remember that, where known, telephone and telex numbers have been included in the manufacturers' index).

Every attempt has been made to ensure accuracy of the details presented in this guide, but doubtless changes will have occurred about which the compilers are unaware. We apologize to any reader to whom we may have given a false lead. A note will be made of up-to-date information which becomes available to ITDG.

It must be stressed that this guide relies on information supplied by the manufacturers and that inclusion of an item is no guarantee of performance. Whilst every care has been taken to ensure the accuracy of the data in this guide, the publishers and compilers cannot accept responsibility for any errors which may have occured. In this connection it should be noted that specifications are subject to change without notice and should be confirmed when making enquiries and placing orders with suppliers.

GENERAL INTRODUCTION

Problems of farmers in developing countries

The main economic characteristic of agriculture in developing countries is the low level of productivity compared with what is technically possible. It has been shown in many and varied circumstances that although farmers may be rational and intelligent, technological stagnation or slow improvements can still be the norm. This contradiction can be explained by understanding several unusual, troublesome features of agriculture. First, because agriculture is basically a biological process, it is subject to the various unique risks of weather, pests and disease which can affect the product supply in an unpredictable fashion. Despite exceptional biological risks, most farmers nowadays rely to various extents upon cash derived from sales of produce. But agricultural products have consumer demand patterns which can turn even good production years — when biological constraints are conquered — into glut years and therefore financial disasters. The biological nature of production also results in a large time-gap, often months or even years, between the expenditure of effort or cash and the returns. Once cash inputs are used, an unusually high proportion of working capital is required, compared with industry. The final problems created by the biological nature of production lie in the marked seasonality. The peaks of labour input create management problems, and perishable commodities are produced intermittently; both create additional financial and technical storage problems.

A second characteristic of agriculture is from the small scale of most farming operations, often coupled with a low standard of education of the operators, which gives farmers little economic power as individuals and little aptitude to seek such remedial measures as do exist. There are many examples of appropriate technology but small farmers will often need intermediaries, such as extension workers and project personnel, to open their eyes to the potentialities. Given the vulnerability of small farmers to biological and economic risks, those intermediaries have special responsibility to assess the impact of any new technology for each particular set of local circumstances.

A third factor which affects efficiency in agriculture is a political one. It is in some ways ironic that in countries with very large numbers of small farmers, producers tend to command little political power despite their combined voting strength. Indeed they are often seen as the group to be directly and indirectly taxed to support other, generally urban-based, state activities. As a contrast, in rich countries, we often see minorities of farmers with little voting power receiving massive state subsidies, much of which supports technological advancement. The rationale of farmers referred to above thus leads to the exploited, small farmers producing well below potential and the rich, large-scale farmers producing food mountains that can only be sold at further subsidized prices.

The 1970s food crisis, the recent failure of agriculture to match rising food demands in many countries, particularly in sub-Sahara Africa, and the failure of industry to fulfil its promise of creating employment and wealth has turned the attention of policy-makers back to the long neglected and often despised agriculture sector. New technology for the large number of low-income, small-scale, poorly educated farmers will be necessary if agriculture's enhanced role is to be successful.

What are the technology options?

Innovation and technology change has been and will be the main engine of agricultural development. Technology

Innovative equipment can be simple in construction: a four-furrow row seeder.

change can be described as the growth of 'know how' (and research as 'know why'). But technology is not just a system of knowledge which can be applied to various elements of agricultural or other production to improve levels or efficiency of output. Technology application requires and uses new inputs. In contrast, technique improvement is the more difficult art of improving production essentially with existing resources. Pity the poor agricultural extension worker sent out to advise experienced farmers with no new technology, but only improvements in technique to demonstrate!

It is possible to exaggerate the lack of prospect for improvement and the consequent need for new investment in farm resource use. Changes both on and off-farm are influencing the economies of traditional systems. For example, with farm size halving every twenty years or so in some regions — as a result of population growth, and with increasing demand for cash from farming activities for production items such as seed (which used to be farm produced) or for consumption items such as radio batteries and so forth, there are new challenges to the traditional rationale and the old system optima. But despite the need to adjust the existing resources to find new optima, the opportunities for really big gains will undoubtedly come from new technology which will often require radically different ways of doing things. A change in the resource base or the injection of a new piece of technology into an interdependent agricultural system may alter various other constraints and opportunities within the overall farm system. One function of a reference book such as this is to act as an encyclopaedia illustrating alternative ways of coping with new challenges. Readers do not have to reinvent the wheel each time a new transport system emerges. Self-reliance has little merit over technology transfer when it comes to solving food availability problems in a rapidly changing world.

This book displays a very wide range of technology and describes both what the technology can achieve, and how and where most information can be discovered. It shows that there is already in existence a mass of tested technology for small-scale farmers. The farm technology itself is laden with opportunities for improving the returns to land, water, labour and other crucial resources. The careful farmer, with help, can have many options.

The role of information

In the theory of classical economics, information on the contents of the technology itself is assumed to be a free good, readily available to all. This is clearly absurd in any industry, but particularly so in agriculture. One of the main justifications for public support of agricultural research and extension, in developed and developing countries alike, is the inability of farmers to search and experiment efficiently and thus to find out what technology is available.

However, knowledge of the existence of appropriate technology will not be sufficient to ensure adoption. Attitudes toward it may need to change, the hardware has to be physically available and those convinced of its value need financial resources to acquire it. One good example of this is family planning technology, where knowledge has generally outrun the capacity of the delivery systems. Similarly, local testing of the appropriateness of various items is very desirable. This in turn, will require more local agricultural research stations to accept responsibility for adaptive research and technology testing. Nevertheless, knowledge is obviously a necessary prerequisite to adoption, and publications such as this have an important part to play in information dissemination.

The impact of technology

Selection of technology for inclusion in this book does not imply endorsement of a particular product. Indeed, supporters of the appropriate technology concept often have an ambivalent attitude to new technology. New technology always changes the system and in particular it is likely to change who benefits from it. Appropriate technology advocates believe the kind of cheap, simple, small-scale, locally produced, reliable or at least mendable technology will increase incomes and improve or at least avoid worsening income distribution. This is possible, but it is still hard to prove that any technology has the ideal intrinsic qualities that will somehow create wealth and at the same time favour the poorest groups in society. On the contrary, experience shows that the income-distribution consequences of change are generally unpredictable. Since new technology normally requires access to resources, it generally favours the better off; the mode of use of technology, and thus its impact, is not a readily visible quality.

To reject all modern technology on grounds related to fears about income distribution is to argue like the elderly man who said that 'if God had meant us to fly He would not have given us railways'. Societies must accept the benefits of new technology and devise means to reduce the social costs associated with any worsening of income distribution — the greater the gain in aggregate income from innovation, the easier this should be to achieve. We are aware that the direct users of the book will seldom be the small farmer client that the contributors and compilers generally have in mind in selecting equipment. But those who have access to this book, such as extension officers, government officials,

Well-designed hand tools can reduce drudgery: harvesting in Morocco.

teachers and local leaders must give guidance with care and with wisdom.

How to choose

In selecting new technology, either for testing or promotion, numerous criteria can be devised to aid judgement. These will include the degree of technical effectiveness, financial profitability, the economic and social returns, health and safety factors, the administrative and legal compatibility with existing conditions. The criteria will not necessarily be independent or even compatible. A financially profitable piece of technology may depend upon underpriced foreign exchange or tax allowances and be economically unattractive. It may substitute capital expenditure on machinery for labour and be socially unattractive. A particular criterion such as technical efficiency, may have several elements to aid judgement — such as the technology's simplicity and labour-intensity, its ecological appropriateness, its scale and flexibility, its complementarity with existing technology and so forth. These elements are not inherently equal and in some circumstances one will be regarded as carrying most weight, in other circumstances another. Choice of technology is a matter of judgement and all the modern aids for technology assessment, for cost-benefit analysis and the like cannot hide this fact. Analysis is an aid to and not a substitute for judgement; the social consequences — which are agonising — must be weighed against the various real benefits that are apparent.

The technologies presented in this book reflect the belief that whilst all technology will alter the economic status of large numbers of people (often in the direction of greater inequality of income, greater commercialization, more wage labour and increasing landlessness) some technologies are more likely to do so than others. You will find few tractors or combine harvesters in this book, for example, but great emphasis on, for example, animal-drawn tool-bars and powered threshers. Technology varies in its degree of reach-down to the low-income farming groups who, if they are not the main target of rural development, are from our viewpoint a key component. The cost of lost output through using less efficient equipment — hand pumps rather than tube-wells, resistant seed rather than crop protection, hand tools rather than tractors, small livestock rather than cattle and buffaloes — is small. Indeed, the productivity of labour-intensive gardening and allotments can often exceed that of modern capital-intensive farming systems — as was shown in Britain during and after the Second World War. Whilst situations do occur where demand for increased food supplies force governments to chase home-produced food without too much thought about the social impact of the production system, such dire circumstances are rare. They might occur where the bulk of low-income people are food purchasers — urban dwellers and landless rural labourers, and in these cases large-scale, capital-intensive state or private farming with the most modern technology, might be justified. But it is only rarely that the trade-off between technical and economic efficiency and equity criteria is painful. Research in many countries has shown that modernized peasant-based systems are generally equally or more efficient and to most views more equitable, and thus it is the small farmers who are seen as the main beneficiaries of *Tools for Agriculture* — even if they are unlikely themselves to be the main readers of this book.

Feedback

Whilst there are a number of people who know and understand the hardware described in this book, there is less understanding of the ways in which technologies are 'delivered', or options presented to the small farmers themselves. ITDG is therefore always pleased to have critical and appreciative feedback — from the aid agencies, extension workers, credit agencies, schoolteachers, businessmen, politicians and others who use this text, on the content and format, equipment that is missing, new problems, the effectiveness of the equipment, the service of the manufacturers, and new ideas for delivery. The hardware available grows rapidly in diversity and power, but, just like computers, it will be useless without the software support. In the case of agriculture, technology software stems from the efforts of interested individuals and groups who are close to the small farmers. We look forward to hearing from you!

Ian Carruthers
Wye College, University of London

Modern technology is easily applied, if one has the resources: fertilizing maize.

HARVESTING AND THRESHING

Harvesting a peasant's smallholding in Peru.

The crop harvesting equipment available to small farmers in the developing countries has changed very little over the years. Knives, sickles and scythes continue to be the traditional tools used to harvest crops. Some low-horsepower reapers are being developed, but because of their low field capacity, high cost and other problems, they are often not considered a suitable alternative to the manual methods. On the other hand, a large number of efficient, low-cost hand, foot or power-driven threshers have been developed for use on small farms around the world.

The search for more efficient, cost-effective ways of harvesting and threshing crops is important because of the extreme labour intensity of these tasks. For example, in developing countries, up to 40 per cent of the total labour required to grow a crop is expended in the harvesting and threshing operations. At peak harvest periods labour shortages often occur, even in regions that normally have surplus labour, and this can lead to higher costs of production or reduced yields (because of the delayed harvesting). It should be remembered, however, that the introduction of new equipment can mean the loss of local employment opportunities.

TECHNICAL CHARACTERISTICS

Harvesting equipment

There are three main types of harvesting equipment: manual, animal-powered, and engine-powered.

Manual

A variety of knives, sickles, scythes and reaping hooks are still the principal tools used by small farmers in the developing countries. They are used to harvest the entire

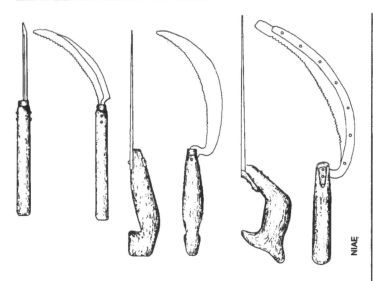

Traditional sickles.

plant or, if necessary, can be used selectively to remove mature plants or seed heads in crops that are not uniformly ripe. The cost of such tools is minimal, they are easily maintained or repaired, and they are familiar and dependable. Manual harvesting is, of course, very labour-intensive and in many situations is an important means of providing work to landless labourers who would otherwise be unemployed.

As harvesters, and in particular threshers, are often paid a percentage of the crop, the value of the wage to the recipient is considerably higher than the cost to the farmer, and may be the labourers' main source of food for the coming year.

Knives A variety of knives are used for cutting plant stalks or grain heads of crops like millet, sorghum and rice. Losses from crop shattering are lower when knife blades are used but labour requirements are very high — about 75 per cent above sickle harvesting. One of the main advantages comes at the threshing stage: selective cutting reduces the moisture content and extra green matter, allowing for safer storage and easier transport.

Sickles A wide range of sickles is used to harvest the majority of cereals and pulses in developing countries. Basically they consist of a metal blade, usually curved, attached to a wooden handle. The degree of curvature and length of blade, the angle of attachment, and the shape of the handle all vary from area to area. The labour requirements for the sickle harvesting vary according to the yield, variety, and moisture content of the straw, and the operators' ability, etc. but are likely to be in the range of 100 to 175 man-hours per hectare. The advantages of harvesting with sickles tend to be greatest with heavy crops.

Scythes A scythe is a curved blade, usually 70 to 100cm long connected to a long shaft which has two handles. The blade is linked to the shaft in various ways, some allowing adjustment of the angle between the two for different crop conditions: the greater the angle the more material is cut at each stroke (and the more arduous the operation). Scythes are efficient harvesting tools, but require considerable skill to use properly.

For cereal harvesting a cradle attachment collects the cut crop and allows it to be deposited at the end of the stroke. The most common arrangement is a group of four or five wooden fingers parallel to the blade. Paddy is not normally scythed as rice straw is both softer and tougher

than wheat straw and more prone to lodging. However, in a good stand of wheat, scything can reduce the labour to between ⅓ and ¼ of that needed for sickle harvesting.

Reaping hooks The reaping hook is a compromise between a sickle and scythe. It is short handled and has to be used in a crouching position, but the sharp blade will cut the crop without having to hold it. Reaping hooks are frequently used with hooked sticks to gather the crop as it is cut.

Animal-powered

Animal-powered harvesters are relatively rare in developing countries. Ox-drawn reapers, based upon designs of machines used with horses, have been tried in India but are not used widely. The limited draught available from ox-pairs, the problems of harvesting lodged crops and the cost of the machines compared to tractor-drawn harvesters, have limited the commercial development of such harvesters.

Engine-powered

A number of prototype reapers and reaper-binders have been designed to meet the harvesting needs in developing countries. In the case of binders, the high cost of twine (estimated at $15/ha) has made certain machines uneconomic. Other harvesters, because of low field capacity, high cost or other problems have, on the whole, been found unsuitable. However, a Chinese vertical conveyor reaper promoted by IRRI is proving to be an efficient mechanical harvester of crops under conditions existing in developing countries.

Threshing equipment

Threshing equipment involves three quite distinct operations:
— separating the grain from the panicle
— sorting the grain from the straw
— winnowing the chaff from the grain.
The first of these requires considerable energy and is the first to be mechanized. Sorting the grain from the straw is relatively easy but is the most difficult stage to mechanize. Winnowing is relatively easy, whether by machine or by hand.

Manual threshing

Most manual threshing methods use some implement to separate the grain from the ears and straw. The simplest

Traditional threshing equipment: a box with threshing bars placed over it and (inset) a flail.

method is a stick or hinged flail with which the crop, spread on the floor, is beaten repeatedly. Such tools are simple and cheap, but they are also slow and exhausting to operate. Rice is usually threshed by beating bunches of panicles against the ground, a stone, a bamboo frame, or the edge of a tub or basket. A screen usually surrounds the threshing area to avoid grain loss. Output per man-hour varies considerably, but is generally between 25 and 50 man-hours per tonne.

Slightly more complex mechanical threshers and shellers are available which still rely only on human power. Treadle-operated threshers, consisting of a drum with rows of wire teeth which is rotated by pedalling a treadle, are commonly used for rice. Output is typically 100-150kg per hour for one-man machines. Such threshers are relatively cheap, light and easily manufactured locally. Because of the higher power requirement, these machines are not suitable for threshing wheat.

Maize shellers consist of a feeder funnel and a shelling disc which is rotated by a hand-crank. The grain is removed as the cob moves down through the machine; output is 100-150kg per hour. Work rates of 750-900kg per hour are claimed for a pedal-operated maize sheller which has a fan to separate light trash from the grain. At an even simpler level are low-cost hand-held maize shellers. These have low work rates but save wear and tear on the hands.

Animal-powered threshing

Animal trampling remains the standard method of threshing grain crops in many parts of the world. While slow, and often resulting in impurities and damage to the grain, it makes threshing less arduous and can be cheap if oxen or buffaloes are readily available. Productivity, at 30-50 man-hours per tonne, is about the same as for manual methods. The animals may pull a heavy object or implement behind them, such as a stone roller, sledge or disc harrows, to increase the rate of work.

Engine-powered threshing

Tractor-treading One method of threshing which has become widespread for rice, wheat, barley and sorghum is driving a tractor round and round on the crop spread over the threshing floor. If tyre pressure is kept low to minimize grain damage, excellent results are possible, and no added investment in machinery is required.

Hold-on threshers In areas where whole, undamaged straw is valued, some machines thresh rice by stripping grain from the panicles without damaging the straw. The simplest of these are mechanized versions of the treadle thresher in which the drum is rotated by a 1-3hp engine. Double drum threshers contain two-wire looped cylinders. Most threshing is done in the slower, first cylinder which strips the grain on the panicles from the straw. The second, faster, cylinder is designed to thresh the broken panicles. Double drum threshers are used for wheat and sorghum as well as paddy. Some have a self-feeding mechanism which continuously feeds the bundles into the machine, thus reducing the labour requirement.

Hold-on threshers require that the crop be formed up into even bundles, and this can be laborious if the crop was badly lodged or if even bundles were not harvested in the first place. Their main advantage is that they solve the major problem of all other threshers — how to separate the grain from the straw.

Through-flow threshers The entire harvested crop is fed into this type of thresher, thus increasing the bulk which has to pass through the machine. Faster feeding is possible but higher power requirements are inevitable. There are two main types:
—Tangential flow machines in which the crop passes directly through the threshing cylinder, around the circumference of the drum.
—Axial flow machines which have spirally positioned fins on the upper concave so that material fed in at one end of the drum passes along the drum as it is rotated, and is ejected at the other end.
In both machines the threshing occurs as the crop passes between a revolving cylinder and a metal grate called the concave, which covers part of the circumference of the drum. Threshed grain falls through the holes in the concave. The mechanism which causes the beating/rubbing which separates grain from straw and chaff can be of several types: wire loop, spike (or peg) tooth, rasp bar, angle bar.

Power for engine-driven threshers may be from a small engine mounted on the machine (2 or 3hp upwards), or from a tractor. Most machines allow adjustments for

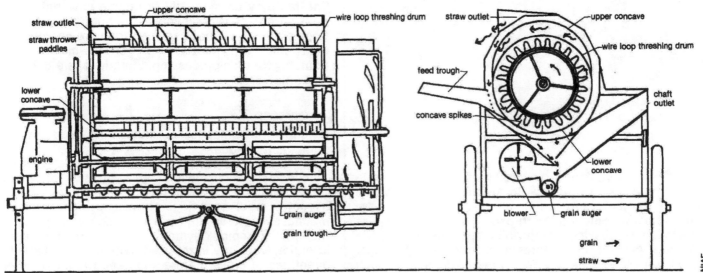

Schematic drawing of an axial flow thresher.

various crop and field conditions, and a large selection is available with varying drum, power supply and winnowing/cleaning arrangements. The simplest consist of little more than the threshing cylinder and concave mounted on a metal framework including feeding chute,

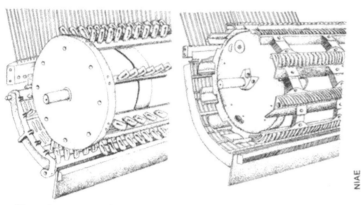

Threshing mechanisms: peg-tooth drum and slotted metal concave (left); Rasp bar and wire concave (right).

More complex threshers which include winnowing fans and sieves to separate grain from straw and chaff include the axial flow thresher developed by IRRI in the Philippines which has been widely adopted by rice producers. Also, the Alvan Blanch Minor thresher from the UK performs successfully with wheat, barley and sorghum; and various Indian-manufactured threshers are used primarily for wheat threshing. They are capable of very high outputs (0.5 to 2 or more tonnes per hour) and remove the need for hand winnowing, but are considerably more expensive and more difficult to repair in rural areas. They are more suitable for contractor operators than individual farmers in developing countries.

Engine-powered threshing in Bolivia.

Maize shellers Engine-powered maize shellers operate similarly to the threshers, with rotating cylinders of the peg or bar type and metal concaves. Cobs must be husked before entering the threshing drum. Some maize shellers have husking rollers which husk the cobs before they are passed to the threshing drum. As with other grain threshers, cleaning fans may be included which remove any trash from the grain. Shellers may have their own engine or be driven from a tractor pto, and range in

size from 1hp models with 100kg/hr capacity to pto-driven models with a capacity of several tonnes/hr.

Separating grain from straw

The simplest way to separate grain from straw is to pick the straw up and shake it, letting the grain fall out. A better method is to use a pitchfork to do the shaking. The earliest mechanical sorters emulated the pitch fork, and this type consists of three or five troughs mounted on cranks in such a way that the straw is picked up and thrown forward by each trough in turn. This is a very simple and reliable mechanism, but it is also very bulky.

With a well-designed threshing drum, roughly 80 per cent of the grain should be sorted in the drum by passing through holes in the concave. Recent developments with axial flow threshers have increased this to 100 per cent so that a thresher can do without the very bulky straw walkers. One feature of the axial flow drum is that sorting is more effective at high loadings, whereas the efficiency of straw walkers falls off very rapidly as the throughput rises. For hand-fed machines, where feeding tends to be erratic, the straw walker is probably the most efficient.

Winnowing

Traditional threshing methods leave a lot of trash among the grain and separating this can require almost as much labour as the original threshing. If there is plenty of wind, the threshed material is tossed in the air using forks, shovels, baskets, etc. (see Section 9 for information on hand tools for materials handling) and the lighter chaff and straw is blown to one side while the grain falls vertically. Final cleaning may be done with a winnowing basket, which is shaken until any chaff and dirt separate at the upper edge. This is very simple and effective but, at only about 40-45kg per hour, it is slow. An alternative is to use winnowing sieves, open weave baskets that may be suspended on tripods. They are shaken so that the grain falls through; the chaff and straw remain in the sieve.

Various types of winnowing machines are designed to create artificial wind. The simplest are hand- and pedal-operated fans: two, three or four light metal blades are rotated by hand cranks or foot pedals. Slightly more sophisticated is the fanning mill, where the fan is mounted in a wooden housing which contains sieves and screens — the grain is thus graded as well as cleaned. The fan may be manually or engine powered. Fanning mills produce a very clean sample but cannot cope with large amounts of straw, so they are more appropriate for finer winnowing. Details of further cleaners, used primarily for crop-processing operations, are to be found in Section 8.

Advantages

Potential advantages of harvesting and threshing equipment include:
● eliminating the labour bottlenecks at peak periods;
● increased yields due to timely cultivation for next crop;
Mechanical harvesting and threshing of crops becomes most advantageous where improved farming practices such as the use of high-yielding varieties, multiple cropping systems and expanded use of irrigation water are introduced. With such systems large quantities of crops mature and need to be harvested at one time, the time for preparation of the land and re-planting of successive crops can be short and, often,

labour for manual harvesting is not available during the peak times when it is needed. With higher yields from better production technology, the relative benefits of mechanical over manual harvesting are increased.

Alternatives

Combined harvester threshers (combines) are the norm for large-scale farms, but they cannot easily be reduced in size and complexity for small farmers. Some work is being done on simple wholecrop harvesters where the crop is cut, and either chopped into short (20-50mm) lengths that in effect threshes it, or else the straw is bruised and broken by drums to give a material which can be used as animal feed. The other approach that shows some hope for the small farmer is the stripper harvester that separates the grain from the ears without cutting the straw. This makes for a very cheap, simple machine.

COSTS AND BENEFITS

Indicative costs

The cost of harvesting and threshing is normally expressed as cost per hectare of crop or as cost per tonne of grain produced i.e. it can be calculated on either an area or weight basis. The total operating cost per hectare is the sum of the total fixed cost of the machine, namely interest, depreciation, tax and repairs and total variable cost which comprises the cost of unskilled and skilled labour, fuel, oil, lubricants. In the case of binders, the cost of binding twine is added to the variable cost.

In the following table, indicative figures are given for the capital costs of a variety of mechanical harvesting devices.

Type		Capital Cost ($)
Mometora Reaper (5hp)	Reaper	693
	Power Tiller	1386
TNAU Reaper (10hp)	Reaper	590
	Power tiller	2250
Satoh Reaper (5.4hp)	Self-propelled machine	1400
Vertical Conveyor Reaper (8hp)	Reaper	1000
	Power Tiller	1750

Source: RNAM (1983)

Economics and scale

Several factors other than capital costs affect decisions on using harvesting and threshing equipment. The size of the farm in physical and economic terms influences the scale of machinery and the size of investment that is appropriate. If only a small amount of work is undertaken each season, then the capital costs per unit of work done may be so high that a machine is uneconomic compared to alternative methods. This can be avoided where multi-farm use is possible, but this use requires a high degree of organization and co-operation, especially where timeliness is critical.

Small and irregularly shaped fields result in low field efficiency of engine-powered or even animal-drawn machines. Poor access increases the time needed to get to the fields, and lack of access roads sometimes

Manual harvesting provides paid employment to some of the poorest members of society.

excludes engine-powered machines altogether. Where terraced cultivation is practised, all tools may have to be light enough to be carried on a person's back.

Traditional cropping systems may exclude or make difficult certain types of harvesting technology. Mixed cropping makes mechanized harvesting difficult. Growing a mixture of varieties of single crop can have the same effect e.g. mixed millet varieties may not all thresh well at a single concave setting and drum speed. Poor land clearing leaving stumps and rocks in the field may prevent the use of animal-drawn and engine-powered implements. Similarly, broadcast or randomly transplanted rice crops cannot always be harvested by machines which rely on crops being grown in rows. These are all factors which must be taken into consideration when deciding to invest in a particular piece of equipment.

Bearing these factors in mind, an example is given of how the cost of harvesting with a 5hp Mometora reaper was worked out in various countries (see page 120).

These costs can be compared with costs of manual harvesting as follows:

	India (rice)	Indonesia (rice)	Pakistan (wheat)	Philippines (rice)	Thailand (rice)
Total cost per hectare $	28	29	31.25	65.76	59
Total cost per tonne $	7	7.25	7.81	16.44	14.75

Health and safety

Much harvesting and threshing equipment is potentially dangerous if not manufactured to an adequate standard or not used properly. Costs of locally manufactured equipment are sometimes kept low by omitting safety features. In India, for example, small town artisans are producing threshers without the protective guard needed to take wheat into the machine and keep hands and arms out. This saves sheet metal but raises accident rates — 95 per cent of which occur while crops are being fed into the machines. With the numbers of new machines increasing by 50,000 per annum, the accident rates during threshing are also rising — from 500 in 1975 to 5000 in 1980.

Fixed and operating costs of harvesting with a 5 hp Mometora. (RNAM 1983.)

A. Fixed Cost ($)

	Reaper	Power Tiller
1. Purchase Cost (p) ($)	693	1386
2. Fixed cost* per hour ($ per hour)		
a) Depreciation	0.30	0.16
b) Interest (12%)	0.15	0.09
c) Repair (8% of purchase price)	0.18	0.11
d) Tax, insurance, housing (2% of purchase price)	0.05	0.03
Fixed cost per hour	0.68	0.39
3. Total fixed cost (for reaper and power tiller per hour)	1.07	

* Assumes 2100 hours and 7 years of life for harvester and 8000 hours and 8 years life for mounting tractor.

Social impact

The introduction of harvesting and threshing equipment can and does lead to displacement from paid employment of some of the poorest sectors of society unless used in circumstances where they permit higher cropping intensities or yields, thus creating alternative work opportunities in other farm activities.

In circumstances where the introduction of such equipment seems desirable from the point of view of the farmer, the employment and equity effects can be taken into consideration by enabling landless workers to purchase machinery through a credit scheme so as to run custom services. This type of scheme is being successfully implemented by various agencies in Bangladesh which have helped groups of landless men and women to benefit from the introduction of pedal threshers rather than be disadvantaged by them.

Ian Johnson
National Institute of Agricultural Engineering

Reference:
RNAM (1983) *Testing, Evaluation and Modification of Cereal Harvesters. Technical Series No.14* Regional Network of Agricultural Machinery of the Economic and Social Commission for Asia and the Pacific. September 1983.

B. Operating cost per ha and per tonne of grain.

Prototype		India	Indonesia	Pakistan	Philippines	Thailand	Thailand
				Mometora (Original)			Mometora (Modified)
Country where tested		India	Indonesia	Pakistan	Philippines	Thailand	Thailand
Crop		Rice	Rice	Wheat	Rice	Rice	Rice
Capacity	hr/ha	15.9	15.6	13.2	12.5	10.5	10.0
Yield	t/ha	2.50	4.00	3.86	5.23	3.65	3.16
Grain loss	%	10.7	14.3	10.5	4.87	3.0	4.8
Labour requirement							
unskilled	man-ha/hr	39.9	162.9	57	64.9	33.5	33.5
skilled	man-hr/ha	16.0	27.8	13	12.5	19	19
Fuel consumption							
gasoline	1/ha	11.5	14.7	13	14.9	13.4	10.2
Price of grain	$/kg	0.15	0.15	0.10	0.15	0.15	0.15
Wage rate							
unskilled	$/day	0.76	0.8	1.01	2.27	2.00	2.00
skilled	$/day	1.9	2.0	2.53	5.68	5.00	5.00
Fuel price							
petrol	$/l	0.5	0.5	0.5	0.5	0.5	0.5
diesel	$/l						
Fixed cost	$/hr	1.07	1.07	1.07	1.07	1.07	1.07
Fixed cost	$/ha	17.00	16.69	14.12	13.38	11.23	10.70
Labour							
unskilled	$/ha	3.79	16.29	7.20	18.42	8.38	8.38
skilled	$/ha	3.80	6.95	4.11	8.88	11.88	11.88
Fuel cost	$/ha	5.75	7.35	6.5	7.45	6.70	5.10
Cost of grain loss	$/ha	40.15	85.80	40.53	38.21	16.43	22.75
Total cost per ha	$/ha	70.50 (30.35)	133.08 (47.28)	72.46 (31.93)	86.34 (48.13)	54.62 (38.19)	58.81 (36.06)
Cost per tonne	$/t	28.20	33.27	18.77	16.51	14.96	18.61

Note: Figures in parentheses are values excluding grain loss. Harvesting losses are extremely difficult to assess accurately. One approach is to estimate the yield by sampling, and then comparing this with the actual amount harvested, but sampling methods can seldom get closer than 2-3 per cent of the true yield, and this is the range of the expected harvesting loss.

The alternative is to try and collect and count the grains on the ground before harvesting (pre-harvest loss) and after harvesting. The problem here is counting the pre-harvest loss without disturbing the crop and causing more loss. With this method of estimating, the result depends to a large extent on the investigator being able to find the lost grain. A good technician will usually record a much higher percentage loss than a lazy one. It is because most people estimate losses in this way in a very casual manner that in general harvesting losses are hopelessly underestimated.

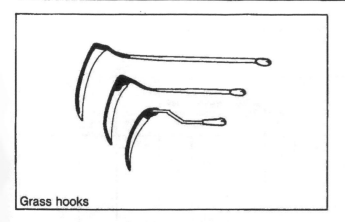
Grass hooks

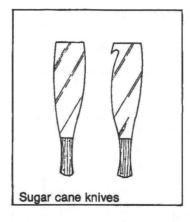
Sugar cane knives

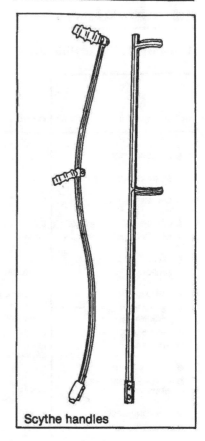
Scythe handles

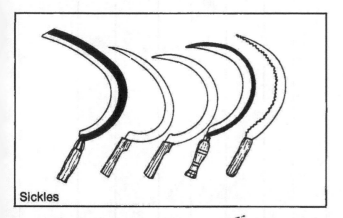
Sickles

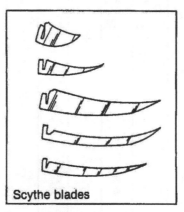
Scythe blades

The use of a sharp blade to cut the plant stem is the simplest form of removing a crop. In each culture a different form of blade has been devised for each type of crop. The most renowned manufacturer of scythes and sickles, Falci from Italy, have dozens of designs specifically tailored to particular markets.

Sickles

The degree of curvature, length of blade, angle of attachment and the shape of handle, vary from area to area and for different crops. A small selection is shown above. Some sickles have serrated edges but there is little evidence to show this to be an improvement.

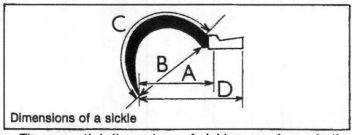
Dimensions of a sickle

The essential dimensions of sickles are shown in the above diagram. 'A' is the length of the implement, including the tang but excluding the handle. 'D' is the total length of the implement. The blade length is measured as the arc 'B' and the development of the blade 'C' is the length around the outer edge, up to but excluding the tang. The other measurement, not shown here, is blade thickness which is the longest width of the blade from outer edge to the sharp edge. Similar measurements are used to describe scythes. In both, the curvature and distance between the plane of the tang or the attachment to the snath (scythe handle) and the plane of the blade, is also noted sometimes by manufacturers: the 'tang height measurement' and (in scythes) the 'tang opening measurement'.

Scythes

These are long curved blades, usually 70 to 100cm long measured along the chord of the blade's arc (similar to dimension A in the drawing on the left), but shorter blades are available for difficult sites (e.g. steep banks). The shaft and handle (snath) designs vary in length and curvature to allow the operator to work with outstretched arms and both hands at approximately the same height from the ground. Scythes can be fitted with a cradle attachment which collects the cut crop and allows it to be deposited at the end of the stroke.

Grass or reaping hooks

These are a compromise between sickle and scythe.

Sugar cane knives

This form of implement has been designed to provide considerable momentum at the point of contact with the sugar cane stem. Often there is a hook on the back of the knife with which the cane is picked up for stacking or chopping into short lengths.

Explanation of table

The table overleaf lists the names of manufacturers of sickles, scythes and sugar cane knives, and the countries from which they come. The following columns give the number of different models of a specific type and their range of blade lengths, that is dimension in the drawing above left, the length of the back of the blade in cm. The number of sugar cane knives manufactured with hooks (h) or non-hooked (nh) is given. The length of handle of the long-handled grass hooks is given as well as their blade lengths. The following columns give the number of different types of scythe handles usually available, the number of different scythe blades manufactured, and their range of lengths.

Table of sickle, scythe and sugar cane knife manufacturers

Manufacturer	Country	Plain Sickle	Length cm	Serrated Sickle	Length cm	Sugar Cane Knife	Length cm	Short Grass Hook	Length cm	Long-Handled Grass Hook	Handle Length cm	Blade Length cm	Scythe Handles	Scythe Blade	Range of Blade Length cm
BULLDOG TOOLS	U.K.	4						1		2					
BURGON & BALL LTD.	U.K.	2	56 59					1		1			1	1	
CALDWELLS LTD.	U.K.	6	48-58	3	48-58	1h		1					1	1	
COLUMBIAN CUTLERY CO.	U.S.A.	4	35 c					2		2	90 130	45			
EICHER GOODEARTH LTD.	INDIA	1		1											
FALCI	ITALY	90	24-44	38				6		2				84	40-80
FERFOR	PORTUGAL	2													
HERRAGUA	GUATEMALA					1h 1nh	35								
HERRAMIENTAS AGRICOLAS NACIONALES	ECUADOR					1h	37								
T. & J. HUTTON CO. LTD.	U.K.			3	52										
IMACASA	EL SALVADOR					1h									
JENKS & CATTELL LTD.	U.K.							1		1					
KENYA ENGINEERING INDUSTRIES	KENYA					1h	52								
KUMAON NURSERY	INDIA	2	40 45	2	40 45	1nh	30								
KUMAR INDUSTRIES	INDIA					1nh	35								
LYSBRO FABRIKER A-S	DENMARK												1	3	65-95
MAHARASHTRA AGRO-IND. DEVELOPMENT CORP.	INDIA					1h									
MODERN ENGINEERING COMPANY	INDIA			1											
AB NORBERGS SPAD & REDSKAPSFABRIKER	SWEDEN											3	6	9	51-74
RALPH MARTINDALE & CO.	U.K.					3h 3nh	28-37								
SANDVIK AB	SWEDEN			2	45-50			1	30				1	2	55 65
SEYMOUR MANUFACTURING COMPANY	U.S.A.	2		2				2	30	2	110 120	30 40	2	5	40-85
S.I.C.F.O.	FRANCE			1	45								1	2	50 65
A. SPALDING & SON LTD.	U.K.									1			1	3	
SPEAR & JACKSON LTD.	U.K.	7	33-39					1	30	1	89	30	1	5	60-91
SYNDICAT DE L'OUTILLAGE AGRICOLE ET HORTICOLE	FRANCE	1		1											
TRAMONTINA SA	BRAZIL	4	25-27							1		22			
TROPIC	CAMEROON					1nh									
W. TYZACK SONS & TURNER PLC.	U.K.							1		2	91 107	32 40	3	13	60-100
WOLF & BANGERT	W. GERMANY					5nh 12h	27-37								
ZANA ZA KILIMO LTD.	TANZANIA	1													

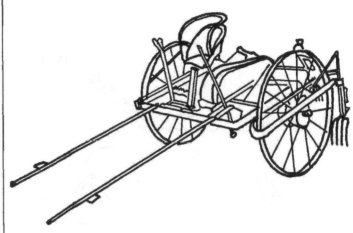

ANIMAL-POWERED GRASS CUTTER

The model 9G-1.4 grass cutter is drawn by two horses and used mainly for mowing grass, other forages, reeds and similar crops. It is suitable for small areas.

Technical specifications:

length	5.03m
width	2.87m
cutting width	1.37m
height of cut	53mm
capacity	3.3 ha/h
weight	328kg.

Manufactured by the Stock Raising Machinery Factory, Hailar City and available through:

CHINA NATIONAL AGRICULTURAL MACHINERY
Import and Export Corporation
26 South Yeutan Street, Beijing
CHINA

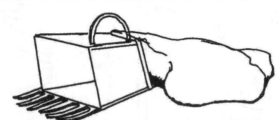

BUFFEL GRASS SEED HARVESTER

A simple tool for harvesting matured buffel grass seed in the standing crop. It is available in two models. Model 1 is smaller and consists of a box with 6 prongs, a handle and collecting bag. It has a capacity of 20-30kg/day and is used by one person. Model 2 is for use by two people and has a capacity of 60kg/day. The tool requires ⅒ of the time for harvesting grass seeds compared to the hand picking techniques commonly used in many countries.

OFICINA VENCEDORA
Av. sete de Setembro 599
56.300 Petrolina, PE
BRAZIL

Z-208 HORSE-DRAWN HAY TEDDER

The Z-208 is a hay conditioner designed for tedding grass being dried for hay. The two wheels are equipped with latch clutches by means of which the drive is transmitted to the tedding forks. Only one horse is required to drive the implement even under very hard field conditions.

Technical specifications:

no. of tedding forks	6
working width	2.1m
capacity	0.6-0.8ha/h
wheel diameter	1m
weight	270kg

Manufactured by Powogaz, Pila and available through:

AGROMET MOTOIMPORT
Foreign Trade Enterprise
P.O. Box 990, Warsaw
POLAND

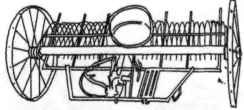

Z-204 HORSE-DRAWN RAKE

The versatile Z-204 horse-drawn rake is designed for raking hay into rows for drying, and raking all crop remnants left on the field after harvest. It can be used for raking potato leaves and branches. The rake consists of the front frame, rake tine assembly and ground wheels. All assemblies are mounted on the carrying beam. It is equipped with a driver's seat and 30 main tines and 2 side tines of adjustable height.

Technical specifications:

traction force	1 horse
capacity	1ha/h
working width	2m
length	4m
width	2.6m
weight	205kg

Manufactured by Agromet-Famarol, Stupsk and available through:

AGROMET MOTOIMPORT
Foreign Trade Enterprise
P.O. Box 990, Warsaw
POLAND

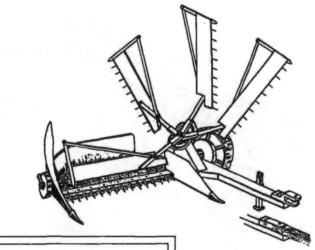

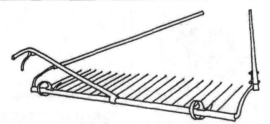

DRAG RAKE

This rake is built for horse-drawn operation and is used for raking grass and hay. It is easy to work with, and has a single handle. For emptying, the lever on the handle is pressed so that the handle drops and grasps the next notch on the pivot at the base of the handle shaft. When the horse pulls, the rake rotates and the teeth rest backwards. When the handle is lifted again the rake rotates to its original position. The teeth are of tempered spring steel, the main frame and handles are made of tubular steel, and the side bars are wooden.

There are six models with working widths ranging from 1.8m to 2.7m, weights from 54 to 59kg, and from 12 to 20 tines.

K.K. LIEN FABRIKK A/S
Tromey, Arendal
4812 Kongshamn
NORWAY

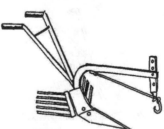

POTATO LISTER

This is an animal-drawn lister with a bent beam, handle and lifting blade with finger mouldboard. It is designed for lifting root crops grown in ridges.

AGRICOLA
34 rue Beni Amar, Casablanca
MOROCCO

SAIL REAPER

The sail reaper is ideal for rice and other cereals. It has a 1.67m wide cutter bar with reciprocating knife. This cuts the crop which falls on the collecting tray and is swept off sideways by the rotating sails clear of the standing crop for tying up by hand. Alternatively it may be followed by a mobile thresher. The machine is available with other cutting widths and as a tractor or animal-drawn implement with optional diesel engine drive. The reaper has a robust construction of good quality steel.

ALVAN BLANCH DEV. CO. LTD.
Chelworth
Malmesbury, Wilts. SN16 9SG
U.K.

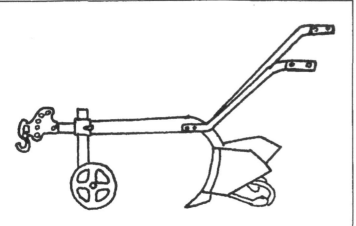

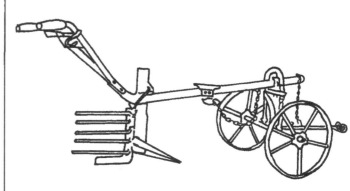

POTATO LISTERS

Agromet Motoimport of Poland export a number of potato harvesting implements. These are known as potato listers, or spinners.

P-418/0 HORSE-DRAWN POTATO LISTER This model (illustrated) is designed generally for earthing up crops planted in ridges, but is also usable for potato harvesting. The lister consists of the central curved body beam to which are attached the handles, digging body and adjustable towing hitch. The latter ensures a correct working depth. The 2 mouldboards of the digging body are mounted on hinges and may be set according to required working width. The lister weighs 20kg.

Manufactured by Wytwórnia Urz. Komunalnych, Kalisz and available through:

AGROMET MOTOIMPORT
Foreign Trade Enterprise
P.O. Box 990, Warsaw
POLAND

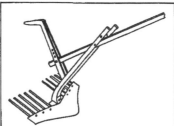

POTATO DIGGER

A simple potato lifting implement designed to be drawn by a single bullock. It has a mean capacity of 0.25ha/day and is able to earth up 98 per cent of the crop, damaging as little as 1 per cent.

GOV. IMPLEMENT FACTORY, M/S
Satya Nagar
Bhubaneswar 75100, Orissa
INDIA

ANIMAL-DRAWN GROUNDNUT LIFTER

Weighing 55kg, this implement is fabricated from easily available forged and cast iron components which may be assembled with the use of a single spanner.

AGRIMAL (MALAWI) LTD.
P.O. Box 143, Blantyre
MALAWI

The Z-402 BEET DIGGER

The Z-402 Beet Digger is designed for earthing up topped and untopped beetroots. Mounted on a 2-wheeled carriage plough frame, it consists of two principal components: 2 digging stumpers and bushes which are welded to the plough frog, and the rear shoe. The rear shoe itself is made up of a 5-rod grid for turning the earthed-up beetroots aside, and is attached to a support bolted to the plough frog. The entire digger is mounted on the central beam of the plough frame by a solid-state yoke and 2 holding bolts. The digger is a single-row implement and requires the equivalent draught of 2 horses and the attendance of 2 workers. It has an average daily field output of 1ha and weighs 20kg (without 2-wheeled carriage plough frame).

Manufactured by Wytwórnia Urz. Komunalnych, Kalisz and available through:

AGROMET MOTOIMPORT
Foreign Trade Enterprise
P.O. Box 990, Warsaw
POLAND

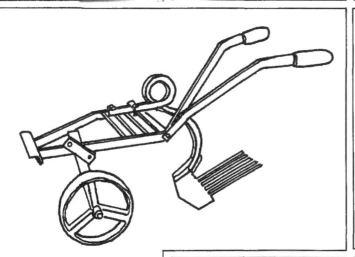

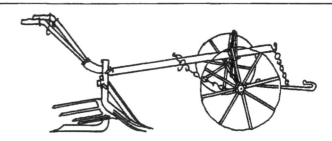

PEANUT DIGGER

Alvan Blanch manufacture the peanut digger illustrated above. It is based on a similar principle to the potato lifters or listers described on this page. It consists of a simple frame to which a ground wheel, handles and digging body are attached.

The digging body comprises a blade which lifts the peanut plants from a depth of about 10-12cm. A finger mouldboard separates the plants from the soil and leaves them upturned on the surface where they are left to dry. This means that the mud on them can easily be removed. The Alvan Blanch peanut digger is designed for animal draught.

ALVAN BLANCH DEV. CO. LTD.
Chelworth
Malmesbury, Wilts. SN16 9SG
U.K.

BEET PLOUGH

This beet plough is essentially similar to that produced in Poland (see above). It is mounted on a 2-wheeled carriage plough frame and requires the draught of 2 horses or bullocks. The digger consists of a curved plough bar or frog to which is attached a 2-finger ridging body. It is also equipped with a coulter and 4 mouldboard fingers which direct the earthed-up beetroots away to the right side of the digger. This is manufactured by Super Tatu S.A. of Brazil and is available through:

TECHNICAL ASSISTANCE
(INTERNATIONAL)
P.O. Box 1224
Vosskuhlenweg 2
2072 Bargteheide
W. GERMANY

CECOCO PEANUT DIGGER

The Cecoco peanut digger lifts peanut plants from a depth of 10-12cm. Two models are available, one for animal draught and the other for power tiller drive (3-6hp). Capacity ranges from 1.2ha/h (animal draught) to 1.5ha/h (power tiller).

CECOCO
P.O. Box 8
Ibaraki City, Osaka 567
JAPAN

THE X-602/0 POTATO SPINNER

The spinner is used to dig out potatoes and to separate them from stalks and soil clods by means of a rotating digging reel. The reel is driven by a gear transmission from the ground wheels.

Manufactured by FMR, Strzelce Opolskie and available through:

AGROMET MOTOIMPORT
Foreign Trade Enterprise
P.O. Box 990, Warsaw
POLAND

SM2 HAND-OPERATED RICE PLANT CUTTER

Used in the same manner as a scythe, this cutter is equipped with scissor blades which are moved by a cable attachment. The cutter handle is steel pipe and the blades are removable for sharpening.

CECOCO
P.O. Box 8
Ibaraki City, Osaka 567
JAPAN

'MOTORSCYTHE' SWATHER

The Motorscythe Swather is a lightweight, heavy-duty rotary cutter suitable for tasks ranging from land clearance to harvesting small cereal plots.

The swather weighs 10kg and is equipped with the following:
- 35cc petrol engine
- shoulder harness
- double-handed control bar
- swathing bat for clearance of standing crops into rows
- tooth whirl blade with guard.

The interested reader is referred to the description of land clearance equipment in Section 13 (Miscellaneous) where a range of brush cutters similar to the 'Motorscythe' is listed.

ALVAN BLANCH DEV. CO. LTD.
Chelworth
Malmesbury, Wilts. SN16 9SG
U.K.

5HP GRASS CUTTERS

Motorized grass cutters in the 5hp range have the advantage of being versatile enough for use in quite difficult terrain, while having sufficient power and capacity for working in quite large areas. The 3 models described here are manufactured in West Germany and Austria and are available for export.

THE AGRIA 5300 This model (illustrated) is able to harvest grass at a rate of up to 0.3ha/h, the Agria 5300 has the following characteristics: combined speed control and engine cut-out mechanism; forward, reverse and idling gears controlled by a single coupling lever; 4-stroke, 5hp petrol engine with recoil starter; pneumatic tyres or cage wheels; independent traction and mowing mechanisms; fingerless 100cm wide cutter bar; total weight 75kg.

AGRIA-WERKE GmbH
Postfach 1147
7108 Möckmühl
W. GERMANY

THE REFORM 115 DIESEL MOTOR MOWER A very sophisticated machine able to carry out a range of tasks in addition to grass cutting. The mower is driven by a Lombardini diesel LDA 520, 4-stroke, 325cc, air-cooled engine which develops 5DIN HP at 3000rpm. It has a fuel consumption of less than 1 litre/h and is equipped with 2 forward and 2 reverse gears. The grass cutting capacity of the 115 motor mower is enhanced by a range of 3 different cutter bars, each suited to certain conditions and grass types. These give cutting widths of 1.4-1.7m. Also available are additional wheel attachments for extra stability (e.g. cage wheels).

REFORM-WERKE BAUER & CO. GmbH
Postfach 192
Haidestraße 40
A-4600 Wels
AUSTRIA

BM 100/2G This mower is the largest of a range of three produced by Gutbrod. It has a cutting width of 100cm and a Gutbrod 2-stroke motor with an output of about 3.7kW.

GUTBROD-WERKE GmbH
Postfach Box 60
6601 Saarbrücken-Bübingen
W. GERMANY

SMALL MOTORIZED GRASS CUTTERS

Alpina manufacture 2 small motorized grass cutters.

THE MODEL HOBBY 202 This consists of a tubular transmission shaft to which is attached the engine, handle-bars, ground wheels and cutter bar mower. It is a lightweight implement (18kg) suited to steep and inaccessible areas of up to 0.2ha. The engine is 2-stroke with an 85cc displacement. This motivates the cutter bar which has an adjustable working height and width of 80cm.

THE MODEL ELITE 402 Although this model (illustrated) is equipped with a similar 85cc, 2-stroke engine and 80cm cutter bar, its heavier construction (25kg) and additional land wheel allow it to be used on large areas. An output of up to 0.1ha/h may be achieved.

ALPINA
31015 Conegliano, Treviso
ITALY

GRASS CUTTERS

The grass cutters described here are similar in form to those of 5HP listed on this page. Their primary function is grass harvesting although they may also be adapted for other mechanized functions. Here, the interested reader requiring information on multi-purpose power tillers, many of which include grass cutter bar attachments, is referred to the relevant pages on motorized tillage in Section 1 of this Guide.

THE MONROTILLER MOTOR SCYTHE This model (illustrated), although designed principally for grass cutting work, may be adapted to perform a range of functions in soil tillage and traction. Accessories include:
- extra diameter pneumatic wheels
- primary tillage equipment
- tool frame attachment
- trailer hitch (sprung or heavy-duty)
- blanking plate for side PTO

MECHGARD LTD.
Great Gransden, Sandy
Bedfordshire SG19 3AY, U.K.

THE BEBY MOTOR SCYTHE An implement with the following technical characteristics:
- 5HP (DIN), 4-stroke petrol engine
- PTO (frontal)
- mowing bar adjustable up to 70cm
- weight 78kg
- spraying pump attachment.

BARBIERI, SpA
Via Circonvallazione, 19
36040 Sossano, Vicenza
ITALY

THE FORMICA 2 M This is similar to the Beby motor scythe, this model has technical specifications which include:
- 5hp, 2-stroke engine
- 2 forward speeds
- adjustable handlebars
- weight 55kg
- lister, trailer and cultivator.

M.A.B. DI GUIDO BOCCHINI
Via Erbosa, 47030 Gatteo (F.O.), ITALY

CAAMS-IRRI 1.6m REAPER

Designed by the International Rice Research Institute (IRRI) in collaboration with the Chinese Academy of Agricultural Mechanisation Sciences (CAAMS), this large reaper is particularly suited to the harvesting of rice.

It has a 6-8hp power requirement and a daily output of approximately 3.8ha. The following gives the reaper's technical specifications: power; 6-8hp petrol engine; gross weight; 255kg; weight of reaper; 77kg; field capacity; 0.38ha/h; field losses; less than 1½; forward speed; 3-5.5kph; fuel consumption; 1.6 litres/h.

F. BUENACOSA REPAIR SHOP
Tacurong, Sultan Kudarat
PHILIPPINES

POYING'S WELDING SHOP
262 National Hi-Way
Brgy. Anos, Los Banos, Laguna
PHILIPPINES

JCCE INDUSTRIES
242 Mayondon
Los Banos, Laguna
PHILIPPINES

CAAMS — IRRI 1.0m REAPER

This motorized reaper has been developed by the International Rice Research Institute in collaboration with the Chinese Academy of Agricultural Mechanization and Sciences.
Technical specifications:
- engine type; petrol:
- power output; 3hp
- labour requirement; 1-3 men
- capacity; 2.4ha/day
- cutting height; 70mm
- speed; 2.5 to 4.5kph
- length of reaper-tiller unit; 2.18m
- weight; 135kg
- fuel consumption; 1 litre/h.

The reaper is produced by the following manufacturers:

ALPHA MACHINERY & ENGINEERING CORP.
P.O. Box 579 MCC
Makati, Metro Manila, D708
PHILIPPINES

B-J ENGINEERING & MACHINE WORKS
1236 Rizal St., San Jose
Baliwag, Bulacan
PHILIPPINES

BORJA MACHINE SHOP
Sgt. de Roma St.
San Pablo City, Laguna
PHILIPPINES

GINTONG ANI METALWORKS
Cainta, Metro Manila
PHILIPPINES

MBP ENGINEERING
KM 16 MacArthur Highway
Malanday, Valenzuela
Metro Manila
PHILIPPINES

POYING'S WELDING SHOP
262 National Hi-Way
Brgy. Anos, Los Banos, Laguna
PHILIPPINES

2M INDUSTRIAL COMPANY
San Mateo, Isabela
PHILIPPINES

F. BUENACOSA REPAIR SHOP
Tacurong, Sultan Kudarat
PHILIPPINES

FELICIANO AGRICULTURAL MACHINERY & WELDING SHOP
Midsayap, North Cotabato
PHILIPPINES

KABACAN ENGINEERING WORKS & SERVICES
Rizal Ave., Kabacan
N. Cotabato
PHILIPPINES

PETER LIMS ENTERPRISES
San Francisco, Agusan del Sur
PHILIPPINES

ROSMAN MACHINE SHOP
Valencia, Bukidnon
PHILIPPINES

MARINAS MACHINERY MAN. CO. INC.
Rizal Street, Pila, Laguna
PHILIPPINES

SWEET POTATO LIFTER

It lifts potatoes grown in ridges and leaves them on the surface of the ground to be picked by hand. It has a lifting depth of 19cm.
Manufactured by the Municipal Institute of Agricultural Machinery, Beijing and available through:

CHINA NATIONAL AGRICULTURAL MACHINERY
Import and Export Corporation
26 South Yeutan Street, Beijing
CHINA

CHINESE HARVESTERS

BEIJING NO. 2 WHEAT AND RICE HARVESTER Designed to be mounted on the front of the Gong Nong 12 walking tractor, this harvester (illustrated) features a vertical table, and a specially designed star wheel lifter instead of a reel. The cut grain is delivered by the conveyor to the right side of the machine to be swathed. Maximum lifting height is 250mm, and minimum cutting height is 60mm.

GANSU 160 WHEAT WINDROWER This machine can be mounted on a 12hp walking tractor and is designed for harvesting wheat crops from 50-120cm high. It has a vertical cutting platform, a reel unit for lifting and a reciprocating cutting bar.
Manufactured by the Tong Xian Harvester Plant, Beijing and available through:

CHINA NATIONAL AGRICULTURAL MACHINERY
Import and Export Corporation
26 South Yeutan Street, Beijing
CHINA

HARVESTER TILLERS

KULIGLIG PALAY HARVESTER Powered by a 3 or 5hp petrol engine, this harvester has a capacity of up to 2.5ha/day. Two people are required to operate it. Overall weight is 150kg, length 250cm, width 118cm

P.I. FARM PRODUCTS
KM 16, Malanday,

Valenzuela, Metro Manila
PHILIPPINES

AGAD REAPER Designed for harvesting paddy, the Agad reaper can be used on wet or dry fields. It requires a 5hp engine and has a capacity of up to 2.4ha/day.

C & B CRAFTS
Maginao, San Rafael, Bulacan
PHILIPPINES

KUBOTA REAPER AR120 This model (illustrated left) has a reciprocating knife bar cutting device, with a cutting height of 10-30cm and a cutting width of 120cm. There is one forward and one reverse gear, with respective speeds of 3.5kph and 3.03kph. The overall weight is 118kg, and power output is 3.4PS (petrol engine). Optional cage wheels are available.

KUBOTA LTD.
2-47 Shikitsuhigashi 1 — Chome
Naniwa-Ku, Osaka 556-91
JAPAN

GRASS CUTTERS

These motorized grass cutters have a power output greater than 5hp. They are equipped with a front cutter bar.

CORTINA/C GRASS CUTTER This model is shown in the illustration with a symetrically attached cutter bar. A lateral version is also available. It has a 10hp petrol or diesel engine with power take-off and 3 speeds, including reverse. Other attachments include a ridger, spray and irrigation pump, plough, trailer and circular saw.

BARBIERI, SpA
Via Circonvallazione, 19
36040 Soasano, Vicenza
ITALY

GRASS CUTTER MODEL 131 Available with either central or lateral cutter bars. The power output is 5, 7, or 9hp, and the gear box provides 3 speeds, 2 forward and 1 reverse. The cutting width is from 650 to 1270mm.

BERTOLINI MACCHINE AGRICOLE, SpA
42100 Reggio Emilia
Via Guicciardi 7
ITALY

790 MOTOR SCYTHE Available with either central or lateral cutter bars. The petrol engine has displacement from 300 to 350cc. At 3600rpm there are 3 forward speeds from 2.3 to 10.2kph and one reverse. Other attachments include: circular saw, compressor, various mowing bars, harvesting attachment, grinder.

O.M. FERRARI, SpA
Via Valbrina 19
42045 Luzzara (R.E.)
ITALY

GRASS CUTTERS MODELS GB 444 and GB 495 The GB 444 has a 4-stroke, 127cc petrol engine. It has a central cutter bar and cutting width of 70cm. The GB 495 is a larger model with a 4-stroke, 161cc engine and cutting width of 110m.

GRANJA, S.A.
109 route de Toulouse
31270 Cugnaux
FRANCE

REFORM 715 MOTOR MOWER Powered by a 4-stroke petrol engine with a power output of 8hp. It has 3 forward speeds from 2.4 to 15km/h and 1 reverse.

REFORM-WERKE BAUER & CO. GmbH
Postfach 192
Haldestraße 40
A-4600 Wels
AUSTRIA

GRASS MOWERS S.E.P. produce a number of machines with either central or lateral cutter bars. Their widths range from 95 to 144cm.

S.E.P.
Fabbrica Macchine Agricole s.r.l.
42016 S. Martino in Rio (RE)
ITALY

A similar 10hp mower with central cutter bar is produced by Pasquali.

PASQUALI SpA
50041 Calenzano (Firenze)
via Nuova, 30
ITALY

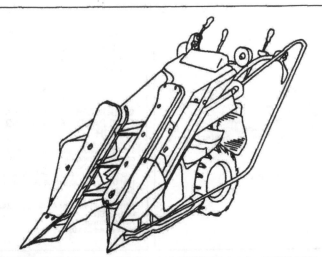

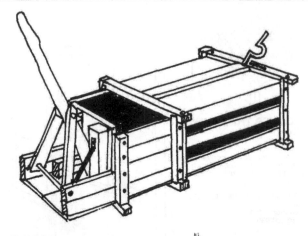

REAPER-BINDERS

Motorized reaper-binders are a development of the more usual power tiller with cutter bar. Although the reaper-binder's cutting width is smaller than that of a cutter bar mower, this is compensated for by the binding mechanism which gathers up the cut grass or cereal, and ties it into sheaves. The latter is a very time-consuming and labour-intensive operation if done by hand alone.

SUZUE BINDERS There are 2 models in this range, the 1-row, 2-wheel Bx300S, and the 2-row, 2-wheel B600DB. The binding is of the knotter and bill type and is carried out with twine.

SUZUE AGRICULTURAL MACHINERY CO. LTD.
144-2 Gomen-cho
Nankoku-shi, Kochi-ken 783
JAPAN

KOREAN BINDERS Listed here are 3 models of binder available for export from Korea. They are the RX-550, KB-602 and HE-50A.

MODEL RX-550: air-cooled petrol engine developing 4.0hp at 4000rpm. It has a weight of 161kg, an average speed of 0.86m/sec, and a cutting width of 50cm. Manufactured by Tong Yang Moolsan Co. Ltd.

MODEL KB-602: air-cooled, 4-stroke petrol engine developing 4.5hp. It has a cutting width of 55cm and a capacity of 4ha/h. Manufactured by Kukje Machinery Co. Ltd.

MODEL HE-50A: a 168kg implement driven by a 4-stroke petrol engine which develops 4.2hp at 3400rpm. An average working speed of 0.85m/sec and working width of 45cm may be expected. Manufactured by Dae Dong Ind. Co. Ltd.
These three binders are all available through:

KOREA TRADE PROMOTION CORPORATION
C.P.O. Box 1621, Seoul
KOREA

HAY BALERS

Equipment for the baling of hay has been devised in most livestock-raising areas where there is concern to maintain production levels during periods of poor pasture production and where there is an excess of forage produced during the growing season. Hay bales are more easily transported than loosely stacked material and, so long as they are tied with resilient twine or with wire, will remain in solid form for a considerable length of time.   Much of the hand-operated equipment is locally made, and consists of a chamber with one or more sides which compress the hay ready for tying.

ENFARDADORA TIPO 1 This simple device (illustrated above) compresses the hay in a small reinforced box of dimensions 72 by 58cm. The length of the compression box is 110cm. By repeated additions of hay to the box a complete bale can be formed.

ENFARDADORA TIPO 2 This more sophisticated baler (illustrated right)

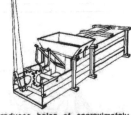

produces bales of approximately the same size but, as can be seen, the feed arrangement and the compression mechanism are different allowing for a more rapid formation of denser bales. There are similar slits in the sides through which the bale twine can be placed.
Construction details for both models available from:

G.I.A.
Ricardo Matte Pérez 0324
Casilla 6122, Correo 22
Santiago
CHILE

TREADLE THRESHERS

Suitable for most types of grain, treadle (often called 'pedal') threshers consist of a frame supporting a peg drum which is rotated on a horizontal axis by a foot-operated treadle board. The sheaves are held close to the pegs on the rotating drum, and the grain is thus separated from the straw. Average outputs from this type of thresher would be in the range of 25-30 kg/h. Treadle threshers are available from the following manufacturers:

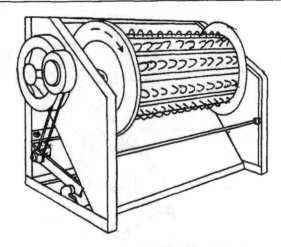

WEST BENGAL AGRO-INDUSTRIES CORPORATION LTD.
23B Netaji Subhas Road
3rd Floor, Calcutta 700 001
INDIA

LIGHT ENGINEERING INDUSTRIES (PTE) LTD.
127 Kottawa Road, Nugegoda
SRI LANKA

RAJAN UNIVERSAL EXPORTS (MFRS) PVT. LTD.
'Raj Buildings'
162 Linghi Chetty Street
Post Bag 250, Madras 600 001
INDIA

KOREA TRADE PROMOTION CORPORATION
C.P.O. Box 1621, Seoul
KOREA

UNION FORGINGS
Focal Point
Sherpur, Ludhiana, Punjab
INDIA

COSSUL & CO. PVT. LTD.
123/367 Industrial Area
Fazalgunj, Kanpur, U.P.
INDIA

AMERICAN SPRING & PRESSING WORKS PVT. LTD.
P.O. Box 7602
Adarsh Housing Society Road
Malad, Bombay 400 064
INDIA

AGRITOM
6 rue de Strasbourg
92600 Asmères
FRANCE

TREADLE THRESHERS

1A RICE THRESHER Equipped with a toothed drum and steel frame, this foot thresher (illustrated) can also be adapted for motor drive. The thresher weighs 100kg, and the drum has a diameter of 420mm and a width of 490mm. A similar heavier (160kg) model is also available from Musuhama.

STANDARD LANDMASCHINEN GmbH
Postfach 1160
3118 Bad Bevensen
W. GERMANY

C.V. MUSUHAMA
Jl. Raya Kajen 248
Tegal, Jawa
INDONESIA

FOOT THRESHER The drum is fitted with steel wire teeth and capacity ranges from 90-130kg/h. Overall weight is 40kg.

CECOCO
P.O. Box 8
Ibaraki City, Osaka 567
JAPAN

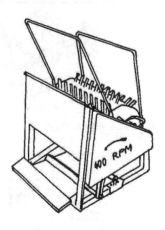

TREADLE THRESHERS

PADDY THRESHER Sismar produce this treadle thresher (illustrated) which can be adapted for motor drive. It has a capacity of 150-250kg/h, and an optional recuperation hood and tub. A similar model is manufactured by Tropic:

SISMAR
B.P. 3214
20 rue Dr. Theze, Dakar
SENEGAL

TROPIC
B.P. 706, Douala
CAMEROON

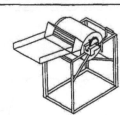

MANUALLY-OPERATED CASTOR THRESHER

This thresher consists of a teak wood cylinder and concave, a feed hopper and an outlet chute, all mounted on an angle-iron frame. The cylinder is rotated by a hand crank.

ANDHRA PRADESH AGRICULTURAL UNIVERSITY
Rajendranagar
Hyderabad 500 030
INDIA

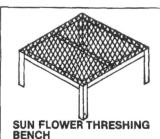

SUN FLOWER THRESHING BENCH

Designed to reduce the time and labour requirements involved in conventional threshing methods. The bench is fabricated from M.S. angle pieces and wire mesh.

ANDHRA PRADESH AGRICULTURAL UNIVERSITY
Rajendranagar
Hyderabad 500 030
INDIA

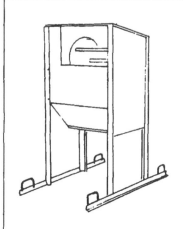

N'DOFFANE GROUNDNUT POD-STRIPPER

This hand-operated groundnut thresher consists of a system of wooden beater bars rotating in a body constructed from angle iron and steel sheet. A table is normally supplied for feeding in the plants. The deflecting sheet is fitted around the beater to allow the nuts to be collected under the machine. The capacity is approximately 200kg/h. The N'Doffane is particularly suitable for stripping undried confectionery groundnuts.

SISMAR
B.P. 3214
20 rue Dr. Theze, Dakar
SENEGAL

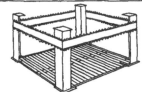

GROUNDNUT POD-STRIPPER CUM PADDY THRESHING BENCH

The goundnuts are drawn against the comb, stripping the pods from the plant and leaving the nuts in the hands of the operators. The device can be inverted so that the grill is uppermost, and used as a paddy thresher.

ANDHRA PRADESH AGRICULTURAL UNIVERSITY
Rajendranagar
Hyderabad 500 030
INDIA

BICYCLE-TYPE THRESHERS

A quite efficient manual threshing method is employed by machines based on the bicycle. One or two operators are required to feed the hopper while providing the power, via a V-pulley, to the threshing mechanism.

THE MINI 'R' PEDAL THRESHER This is suitable for rice and most other cereals (optional accessories available for sorghum). The unit is operated by 2 men. A sloping sieve at the discharge point helps separate the straw from the grain which can be collected in a shallow skip or sheet. The thresher is equipped with twin wheels and has an output of up to 200kg/h.

THE MINI 'M' PEDAL THRESHER This model (illustrated) is similar to the Mini 'R' but designed specifically for threshing millet. This is achieved through rubber beaters operating against steel concave bars over heavy gauge perforations. Output is up to 100kg/h.

Both the Mini 'R' and Mini 'M' threshers may be equipped with a motor, and are available from:

ALVAN BLANCH DEV. CO. LTD.
Chelworth
Malmesbury, Wilts. SN16 9SG
U.K.

THE MIDC PEDAL THRESHER Powered by one person, this implement was developed by the Metal Industries Development Center (MIDC) using locally available materials. It has a total weight of 38kg and an optimum pedal speed of 65rpm.

METAL INDUSTRIES DEV. CENTER
Jalan Sangkuriang 12
P.O. Box 113, Bandung
INDONESIA

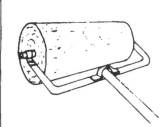

STONE THRESHING ROLLER

This threshing roller is tapered so that it can easily be pulled round in circles over the crop by animals.

DANDEKAR BROTHERS
Sangli-Shivaji Nagar, 416 416
Maharashtra
INDIA

ANIMAL-DRAWN OLPAD THRESHER

This machine comprises serrated discs of 450mm diameter mounted on a steel shaft, and held in position by cast iron spools. The frame is of angle iron and includes a seat with foot and back rest for the operator. Back and front safety guards eliminate the risk of injury to the operator. The harvest is spread on the threshing floor and the machine is drawn round and round, thus separating the grain. An extra raking attachment can be fitted for stirring the straw during the threshing operation. The thresher is available in 20, 14, 11, and 8 disc sizes, weighing 190kg, 125kg, 110kg, and 92kg respectively. Capacity ranges from 350-850kg/day, according to the size of the thresher.

COSSUL & CO. PVT. LTD.
123/367 Industrial Area
Fazalgunj, Kanpur, U.P.
INDIA

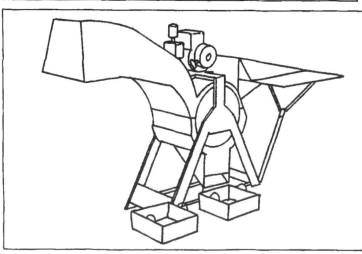

VOTEX RICE FAN

The Votex Rice Fan comprises 30 fan blades and 6 beater bars, collecting trays enabling easy bagging, and a simple v-belt drive suitable for any petrol engine of 3.5-5hp. The Rice Fan can also be fitted with a diesel engine. In this case, a detachable sub-frame, with silent blocks to absorb the extra vibration, and an engine guard can be supplied. The overall weight of the standard model is 127kg; the diesel model weighs 200kg. Although, as its name suggests, the Votex Rice Fan was developed as a rice thresher, with minimal adjustments it can also be used for threshing various other crops such as wheat, barley, oats, cowpeas, sorghum and soybeans.

VOGELENZANG ANDELST B.V.
Postbus 1, 6673 ZG Andelst
Wageningsestraat 30, 6673 DD
HOLLAND

WATKINS NAYLER & CO. LTD.
Friars Street, Hereford
U.K.

ATS MIDGET THRESHER MKII A

Suitable for threshing wheat, barley, oats, beans, peas, sorghum, maize and rice, the Midget consists of a 6 beater, rasp bar drum with sealed bearings. The construction is of heavy plate with a lightweight feed chute and discharge hood over a simple fixed grid straw separator and grain chute. The power required is 3hp and capacity is up to 500kg/h for dry wheat. The overall weight is 127kg. Various concave attachments are available for maize, groundnuts and sorghum, including an extra pulley to reduce the drum speed. A screen separator is also available. Alvan Blanch produce a wide range of threshers, including the larger Master Midget which can be used as a peg drum thresher as well as a rasp bar, making it ideal for threshing high quality rice.

ALVAN BLANCH DEV. CO. LTD.
Chelworth
Malmesbury, Wilts. SN16 9SG
U.K.

IRRI PORTABLE THRESHER TH6

The IRRI portable thresher consists of a metal frame, a pegtooth cylinder with straw throwing paddles on one end and enclosed by a cover with spiral louvres, and a wire mesh or round rod lower concave. A feeding tray, fan for winnowing, removable handle bars for transport and a 5hp petrol engine complete the unit.

Material is loaded onto the tray and fed into the opening between the cylinder and the lower concave. The pegs from the threshing cylinder hit the material, separating the grain from the straw, and at the same time accelerating them around the cylinder. The majority of the grain is threshed during the initial impact but further threshing is performed while the material moves axially until the straw is discharged at the opposite end. Threshed grain including impurities such as leaves and short pieces of straw, pass through the openings in the lower concave where it is cleaned by the winnowing fan. Threshing and separation losses are minimized by the cut-off wall installed at the end of the

lower concave next to the straw thrower and by the stripper bars opposite the feed opening. The cut-off wall prevents grain from going into the straw thrower while the bars cut long straw for ease in axial movement and prevent straw from wrapping around the cylinder during threshing.

Some models of this thresher provide a door in the top cover for hold-on threshing. This threshing method is used in areas where the straw is used for mat and basket weaving. The door is raised and locked in place thereby exposing the entire cylinder length to hold-on threshing.

- power: 5hp engine
- weight (with engine): 105kg
- length: 95cm
- width (with feed tray folded): 76cm
- height (with feed tray folded): 138cm
- capacity: up to 800kg/h (rough rice)
- separation recovery: 98% (weight basis)
- grain purity (without cleaning screen): 94%
- grain breakage: less than 2%
- cylinder: pegtooth, 30.5cm O.D. 71.1cm length

- construction: all steel
- cylinder: 600-630rpm
- fan: engine speed
- labour requirement: 2-3 men
- fuel consumption (approx): 1 litre/h

BORJA MACHINE SHOP
Sgt. de Roma St.
San Pablo City, Laguna
PHILIPPINES

C & B CRAFTS
Maginao, San Rafael, Bulacan
PHILIPPINES

FRECOSA METALCRAFT
San Juan, Calamba, Laguna
PHILIPPINES

GINTONG ANI METALWORKS
Cainta, Metro Manila
PHILIPPINES

ISAROG INDUSTRIES
826 Renacimiento St., Tabuco
Naga City, Camarines Sur
PHILIPPINES

JCCE INDUSTRIES
242 Mayondon
Los Banos, Laguna
PHILIPPINES

KATO INTERNATIONAL
92 P. Santiago Street, Malinta
Valenzuela, Metro Manila
PHILIPPINES

KAUNLARAN INDUSTRIES
Calamba, Laguna
PHILIPPINES

L.P. ENGINEERING SERVICES
San Jose, Baliwag, Bulacan
PHILIPPINES

MECHANICAL FACTORS INC.
Ground Floor
Greenhills Dev. Bldg.
710 Shaw Blvd. Mandaluyong
Metrol Manila
PHILIPPINES

P.I. FARM PRODUCTS
KM 16, Malanday, Valenzuela
Metro Manila
PHILIPPINES

POYING'S WELDING SHOP
262 National Hi-Way
Brgy. Anos, Los Banos, Laguna
PHILIPPINES

SABIO AGRICULTURAL EQUIPMENT
Magarao, Camarines Sur
PHILIPPINES

TECHNO-ADAPTORS INC.
San Isidro
San Fernando, Pampanga
PHILIPPINES

A1 ENTERPRISES
Luna St., La Paz, Iloilo City
PHILIPPINES

APEX FARMERS' SUPPLY
143 Burgos St., Tacloban City
Leyte
PHILIPPINES

BETSY MARKETING
Huervana St., La Paz
Iloilo City
PHILIPPINES

CARVEL ENGINEERING WORKS
Km. 1, Roxas City, Capiz
PHILIPPINES

JAMANDRE INDUSTRIES
88 Rizal St., La Paz
Iloilo City
PHILIPPINES

JASPE METALCRAFT
Evangelista St., Pavia
Iloilo City
PHILIPPINES

MB ENTERPRISES
IPSTA Bldg. La Paz
Iloilo City
PHILIPPINES

V&L AGRICULTURAL MACHINERY
Rizal St., La Paz
Iloilo City
PHILIPPINES

PETE LIMS ENTERPRISES
San Francisco, Agusan del Sur
PHILIPPINES

TRYME AGRO-INDUSTRIES
Lumbia, Pagadian City
PHILIPPINES

ALPHA MACHINERY & ENGINEERING CORP.
P.O. Box 579 MCC
Makati, Metro Manila, D708
PHILIPPINES

F. BUENACOSA REPAIR SHOP
Tacurong, Sultan Kudarat
PHILIPPINES

CECOCO THRESHERS

POWER THRESHER The Cecoco power thresher (illustrated above left) is available in three sizes. The L-15 requires 0.5hp, and has a capacity of 300-350kg/h. It has a width of 45cm. The L-18 is 54cm wide, with a capacity of 400-450kg/h and a power requirement of 0.5hp. The L-20 is 60cm wide, and has a capacity of 500-550 kg/h and a power requirement of 1hp.

UNIVERSAL THRESHER The universal thresher (illustrated above right) is a larger model than the power thresher

above, with a width of 75cm and a power requirement of 2-4hp. It is suitable for threshing various kinds of beans and other pulses, rice and wheat, and features interchangable screens for different sizes of grain. The speed can be adjusted by changing the V-belt pulleys between the threshing drum and winnower. The universal thresher has a capacity of 1500kg/h for beans, and an overall weight of 120kg.

CECOCO
P.O. Box 8
Ibaraki City, Osaka 567
JAPAN

AKSHAT AND AMUDA SEMI-AUTO THRESHERS

American Spring and Pressing Works and Rajan Universal Exports both produce a similar semi-auto, multipurpose thresher. It consists of a threshing chamber, separator, dust discharging device, and a grain conveying and elevating mechanism. The threshing chamber contains a drum with 40 steel wire loops and a concave grill. The heads of grain are inserted into the threshing chamber, where the revolving drum combs out the grain which falls through the grill into the winnowing chamber. Clean grain is raised by the elevator for bagging. The semi-auto thresher has a power requirement of 2hp and a capacity of 200kg/h (rice).

AMERICAN SPRING & PRESSING WORKS PVT. LTD.
P.O. Box 7602
Adarsh Housing Society Road
Malad, Bombay 400 064
INDIA

RAJAN UNIVERSAL EXPORTS (MFRS.) PVT. LTD.
'Raj Buildings'
162 Linghi Chetty Street
Post Bag 250, Madras 600 001
INDIA

PLOT THRESHER

This small thresher was specially developed for threshing different grains in experimental plots. It incorporates a special air device which enables the operator to adjust the air flow ensuring efficient separation of the chaff from the seed. The engine requires 7hp, and the overall weight is 480kg. The thresher is equipped with two tyred wheels and tow bar.

SWANSON MACHINE CO.
20-26 E. Columbia Avenue
Champlain, Illinois 61820
U.S.A.

BENAGRO PADDY-CUM-WHEAT THRESHER 5PW

This machine consists of an all-steel body fitted with a threshing cylinder, screw grain conveyor and a winnower for cleaning. It has an extra threshing bar attachment and blower driver pulley for wheat and paddy. The crop bundle is held with both hands and the heads inserted between the rotating cylinder loops and the concave screen. The separated grain falls through the screen and is cleaned by the winnowing action of air from the blower. The clean grains are finally delivered by means of the screw conveyor to the bag attached to the delivery spout. This machine has a power requirement of 3hp (electric motor) or 5hp (engine), and a capacity of 100-250kg/h for paddy, and 80-125kg/h for wheat.

WEST BENGAL AGRO-INDUSTRIES CORPORATION LTD.
23B Netaji Subhas Road
3rd Floor, Calcutta 700 001
INDIA

POWER-OPERATED CASTOR THRESHER

Consisting of a teak wood cylinder and concave, a feed hopper, a blower, and a 3-sieve assembly. The perforated sheet at the bottom allows sand particles, weed seeds etc. to be sieved out of the shelled castor beans.

ANDHRA PRADESH AGRICULTURAL UNIVERSITY
Rajendranagar
Hyderabad 500 030
INDIA

MULTICROP AXIAL FLOW THRESHER

This is an all-steel, general-purpose thresher suitable for paddy, wheat, sorghum, bajra, soybeans and other small grain or pulse crops. It requires 5-7hp (petrol engine) and has a capacity ranging from 300kg/h for wheat to 600kg/h for sorghum. Overall weight (excluding engine) is approx. 320kg.

AMERICAN SPRING & PRESSING WORKS PVT. LTD.
P.O. Box 7602
Adarsh Housing Society Road
Malad, Bombay 400 064
INDIA

LAKSHMI AXIAL FLOW THRESHER

Suitable for a variety of grains, the Lakshmi thresher combines threshing and winnowing. It has a power requirement of 7hp and a capacity of up to 900-1000kg/h for paddy.

P.M. MADURAI MOODALIAR & SONS
Madural Moodaliar Road
Postbox 7156, Bangalore 560 053
INDIA

STANDARD AXIAL FLOW THRESHER

The Standard axial flow thresher (illustrated) has a power requirement of 10hp. It is suitable for a variety of crops and can be easily converted into a maize sheller. Capacity ranges from 800kg/h for paddy to 2500kg/h for sorghum.

UNION TRACTOR WORKSHOP
8-B Phase 11
Maya puri Industrial Area
New Delhi 110 064
INDIA

IRRI AXIAL FLOW THRESHERS TH7 & TH8

These threshers are essentially large versions of the TH6 axial flow thresher. They are heavier and hence are mounted on a wheeled chassis. The specifications are:

- power: 7hp engine
- weight (with engine): 430kg
- length: 258.45cm
- width: 130.18cm
- height
  with wheel: 158.12cm
  without wheel: 111.76cm
- separation recovery: 98% (weight basis)
- cylinder: spiketooth 39.8cm O.D. × 122.0cm length
- construction: all steel
- component speeds
  cylinder: 500-530rpm
  fan: 1030rpm
- oscillating screen: 334-354 cycles/min
- oscillating screen (stroke): 0.925cm
- adjustments: angle of air deflector and engine speed.

ALPHA MACHINERY & ENGINEERING CORP.
P.O. Box 579 MCC
Makati, Metro Manila, D708
PHILIPPINES

C & B CRAFTS
Maginao, San Rafael, Bulacan
PHILIPPINES

FRECOSA METALCRAFT
San Juan, Calamba, Laguna
PHILIPPINES

JCCE INDUSTRIES
242 Mayondon
Los Banos, Laguna
PHILIPPINES

KASAGANAAN INDUSTRIES
San Jose, Mindoro Occidental
PHILIPPINES

L.P. ENGINEERING SERVICES
San Jose, Baliwag, Bulacan
PHILIPPINES

MECHANICAL FACTORS INC.
Ground Floor
Greenhills Dev. Bldg.
710 Shaw Blvd. Mandaluyong

Metro Manila
PHILIPPINES

P.M. MADURAI MOODALIAR & SONS
Madurai Moodaliar Road
Postbox 7156
Bangalore 560 053
INDIA

NIBROS MANUFACTURING CORP.
Dona Rosario Heights
Novaliches, Metro Manila
PHILIPPINES

P.I. FARM PRODUCTS
KM 16, Maianday
Valenzuela, Metro Manila
PHILIPPINES

POYING'S WELDING SHOP
262 National Hi-Way
Brgy, Anos, Los Banos, Laguna
PHILIPPINES

TECHNO-ADAPTORS INC.
San Isidro
San Fernando, Pampanga
PHILIPPINES

JAMANDRE INDUSTRIES
88 Rizal St., La Paz
Iloilo City
PHILIPPINES

VICMAC CORPORATION
Mandalagan, Bacolod City
Negros Occidental
PHILIPPINES

KATO INTERNATIONAL
92 P. Santiago, Malinta
Valenzuela, Metro Manila
PHILIPPINES

KAUNLARAN INDUSTRIES
Calamba, Laguna
PHILIPPINES

DRUMMY THRESHERS

HIRA THRESHER Fitted with a threshing drum and a fan, this thresher (illustrated left) is available in 4 sizes, ranging from 3-10hp. With the largest model, capacity can reach 4000kg/h.

INTERNATIONAL MFG. CO. (REGD.)
Hospital Road, Jagraon
Ludhiana, Punjab
INDIA

MACO WHEAT DRUMMY THRESHER Three models (illustrated right) are available, with power requirements of 5, 7.5 and 10hp.

MOHINDER & CO. ALLIED INDUSTRIES
Kurali, Distt. Ropar, Punjab
INDIA

K.I.W. DRUMMY TYPE THRESHER Available in a range of models, from 5-15hp.

KHALSA IRON WORKS
2015 Railway Road
Narela, Delhi 110 040
INDIA

JYOTI THRESHERS

WHEAT THRESHER This machine (illustrated) can be adapted for crops other than wheat, by changing the required screens and pulleys. Power requirement is 7.5hp and capacity ranges from 300-500kg/h for wheat, to 1300-1600kg/h for jowar. Overall weight is 535kg.

MULTI-CROP THRESHERS Suitable for all types of grain, this is a light machine with a power requirement of 3hp and a capacity of 150-200kg/h for wheat, 500-800kg/h for jowar. Overall weight is 250kg.

PADDY THRESHER The power required is 5hp and capacity ranges from 300-400kg/h for wheat, to 600-1000kg/h for jowar. Overall weight is 530kg.

JYOTI LTD
Bombay Shopping Centre
R.C. Dutt Road
Vadodara 390 005
INDIA

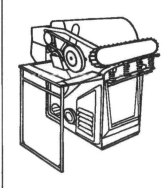

CHINESE AND KOREAN THRESHERS

WP400 THRESHER This small machine (illustrated) is designed primarily for threshing rice and wheat. It has a capacity of 350-750kg/h for wheat and 600-1000kg/h for rice, and a power requirement of 5hp.
Manufactured by the Zhing Jan Thresher Factory and available through:

CHINA NATIONAL AGRICULTURAL MACHINERY
Import and Export Corporation
26 South Yeutan Street, Beijing
CHINA

KOREAN AUTOMATIC THRESHERS Four models are produced in Korea, with a power requirement of 3-5hp. Capacity ranges from 1200kg/h for the smaller models, to 1400kg/h for the larger models.

KOREA TRADE PROMOTION CORPORATION
C.P.O. Box 1621, Seoul
KOREA

MULTI-CROP THRESHER

Threshes wheat, bajra, jawar and other crops with minimum grain loss and breakage. Power required 5hp. Capacity 3-4 quintals/h at 820rpm.

DANDEKAR BROTHERS
Sangli-Shivaji Nagar, 416 416
Maharashtra
INDIA

POWER THRESHERS

AJANTA MULTIPURPOSE THRESHER Several models are available, ranging from 5-50hp. It has tempered adjustable treaded spikes and an adjustable air flow. (Illustrated left).

MOHAN SINGH HARBHAJAN SINGH
G.T. Road,
Goraya 144 409 (Pb.) Distt.
Jullundur (N.R.)
INDIA

K.I.W NEW-TYPE THRESHER WINNOWER

KHALSA IRON WORKS
2015 Railway Road
Narela, Delhi 110 040, INDIA

UT SONA WHEAT THRESHER This thresher (illustrated right) has a power requirement of 10hp, and capacity of 300 kg/h.

UNION TRACTOR WORKSHOP
8-B Phase 11
Maya puri Industrial Area
New Delhi 110 064, INDIA

ROTOR THRESHERS

ROTOR TYPE WHEAT THRESHER This machine (illustrated) is fitted with a spike-tooth threshing drum, and is suitable for threshing a variety of grains. Three models are available, with power requirements of 3-7.5hp, and capacities ranging from 1-4 quintals/h for wheat, to 3-7 quintals/h for jawar.

STANDARD AGRICULTURAL ENGINEERING CO.
824 & 825 Industrial Area B
Ludhiana A-141 003, Punjab
INDIA

MULTIPURPOSE THRESHER Four models are available, with power requirements of 3-10hp.

AMAR AGRICULTURAL IMPLEMENTS WORKS
Amar Street, Gill Road
Janta Nagar, Ludhiana-141003
INDIA

MACO ROTOR TYPE POWER WHEAT THRESHERS These threshers, ranging from 3-15hp, are suitable for threshing wheat, jowar, bajra, sorghum, barley etc.

MOHINDER & CO. ALLIED INDUSTRIES
Kurali, Distt. Ropar, Punjab
INDIA

WHEAT THRESHING AND WINNOWING MACHINE Again, a series of models is available, with power requirements of 5-15hp, and capacity ranging from 2-7 quintals/h.

ALLIED TRADING COMPANY (INDIA)
Railway Road
Ambala City, Haryana
INDIA

HIRA THRESHER AUTOMATIC The Hira automatic comprises a peg type drum, a suction fan and two sieves. Specifications are similar to those of the Allied thresher above.

INTERNATIONAL MFG. CO. (Regd.)
Hospital Road, Jagraon
Ludhiana, Punjab
INDIA

SHERPUR THRESHERS

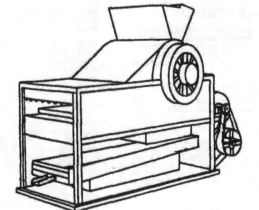

SHERPUR POWER THRESHER WINNOWER This is a versatile machine (illustrated left) suitable for threshing crops such as wheat, barley, millet, soybean, mustard etc. It consists of a spike-tooth cylinder with steel bolts, and a concave mechanism. The cylinder speed for threshing particular crops can be altered either by adjusting the speed of the prime mover, or by the provision of a pulley. Separation of the grain from the straw is achieved by an aspirator and a set of oscillating sieves. The speed of the aspirator and that of the sieves is adjustable. The thresher winnower can be operated with a 5-25hp motor or engine

SHERPUR PADDY THRESHER Designed for threshing both wet and dry paddy, the machine (illustrated right) comprises a spike-tooth cylinder, a concave mechanism and a blower. It has a power requirement of 10-20hp. Capacity ranges from 6-8 quintals/h (using 10hp motor) up to 10-12 quintals/h (using 20hp motor).

UNION FORGINGS
Sherpur, Ludhiana, Punjab
INDIA

PADDY THRESHERS

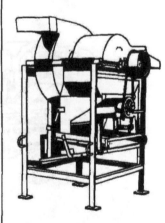

KERTA LAKSANA PADDY THRESHER This machine (illustrated) is constructed of steel plate and is designed for threshing paddy. It consists of a threshing drum with spike tooth cylinder, a separator fan, and a swinging sieve at the bottom. It has a power requirement of 4hp and a capacity of 400-500kg/h. Overall weight is 225kg.

P.T. KERTA LAKSANA
Jl. Jenderal Sudirman 504
Bandung
INDONESIA

BUMA SAKTI PADDY THRESHER An all-steel paddy thresher with a capacity of 300-600kg/h. It can be powered by electric motor or diesel engine. Overall weight is 105kg.

P.T. BUMA SAKTI
Jl. Surfani 8, Bandung
INDONESIA

THRESHERS

BENAGRO POWER-OPERATED WHEAT THRESHER 510 This thresher (illustrated) comprises an all-steel body, fitted with a peg-type threshing cylinder, centrifugal blower assembly, and top and bottom shaker unit. It has a power requirement of 3hp (electric motor) or 5-10hp (diesel engine). Overall weight is 230kg.

WEST BENGAL AGRO-INDUSTRIES CORPORATION LTD.
23B Netaji Subhas Road
3rd Floor, Calcutta 700 001
INDIA

KISAN POWER PADDY THRESHER This is a similar machine for threshing paddy and has a capacity of 300-600kg/h of paddy.

KISAN KRISHI YANTRA UDYOG
64 Moti Bhawan, Collectorganj
Kanpur 208 001
INDIA

TB60 DOUBLE THRESHER

The TB60 thresher has double husking rollers and knife-shaped gears. The knife-shaped gears fixed onto the rotating rollers interact with bow-shaped gears fixed onto the concave board in order to comb and thresh the grains. The threshed grain falls through the gaps while the stalks are thrown upwards by the rotary action of the roll bar. The TB60 has a power requirement of 6-8hp (diesel engine) and 6-7hp (electric motor). It has a capacity of 400-600kg/h for wheat, and 800-1200kg/h for rice, and is suitable for threshing all kinds of large grains. The overall weight is 235kg.

CHINA NATIONAL AGRICULTURAL MACHINERY
Import and Export Corporation
26 South Yeutan Street
Beijing
CHINA

THRESHERS

YANMAR DOUBLE DRUM PADDY THRESHER This rasp bar thresher has a power requirement of 7hp and a capacity of 900-1000kg/h. It weighs 169kg.

P.T. YANMAR AGRI M/G (P.T. YAMINDO)
42 Ji. Ir.H. Juanda
P.O. Box 4135/JKT, Jakarta
INDONESIA

AR 500 A AND AR 1000 A Both threshers have two rasp bar threshing drums. Power requirement is 5 and 8-10hp, capacity 500kg/h and 1000kg/h respectively. The AR 500 A weighs 113kg, the AR 1000 A, 177.5kg.

P.T. AGRINDO
Desa Bambe Kab. Gresik,
Jawa, Timur
INDONESIA

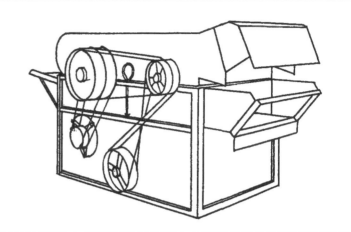

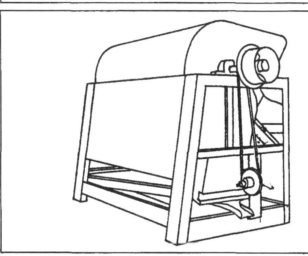

MADHO WHEAT THRESHERS

Madho produce a range of wheat threshers which are also suitable for threshing other crops such as barley, jowar, bajra, pulses etc. It performs the threshing, screening and winnowing processes in one operation.
Technical specifications:

Model	Electric motor hp	Oil engine hp	Output kg/h
1	5	5-8	200
2	7.5	10	300
3	10	12-15	500
4	15	20	600-700
5	20	25	800

MADHO MECHANICAL WORKS
B-49 Industrial Focal Point
G.T. Road
Moga 142 001 (Punjab)
INDIA

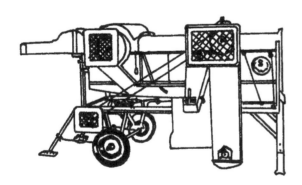

STANDARD THRESHERS

STANDARD UNIVERSAL THRESHER RD IVa This machine (illustrated above) is suitable for threshing all cereals. It consists of a peg-threshing drum and adjustable concaves. It has a power requirement of 5-8hp, and an overall weight of 470kg.

STANDARD RICE THRESHER IIa Adaptable for hand, foot or motor drive, this thresher is equipped with a toothed drum and toothed concave. It does not have a cleaner and straw shaker attachments. Power requirement is 3-5 hp, and overall weight is 330kg. (illustrated below).

STANDARD GmbH
Postfach 1160
3118 Bad Bevensen
W. GERMANY

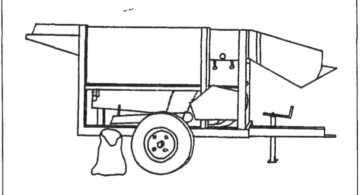

MOBILE THRESHERS

AMAR MULTICROP THRESHER This is a raspbar thresher suitable for all cereals, soybeans etc. It requires 10hp, and has a capacity of 6-10 quintals/h for wheat, and 25-35 quintals/h for maize. The overall weight is 640kg.

AMAR AGRICULTURAL IMPLEMENTS WORKS
Amar Street, Gill Road
Janta Nagar, Ludhiana-141003
INDIA

VICON THRESHER ST-45 The ST-45 is fitted with a rasp bar drum, and can be equipped with wheels for trailing, or a yoke for bullock draught. It has a power requirement of 10hp, and a capacity ranging from 1000kg/h for wheat, to 2000kg/h for maize. The overall weight is 790kg.

VICON LTD.
K.R. Puram — Whitefield Road

Mahadevapura Post
Bangalore 560 048, Karnataka
INDIA

MINORETTE AND MINOR THRESHERS The minorette (illustrated) has a power requirement of 7.5hp. It can be fitted with either a peg drum, consisting of 12 bars each with 5 pegs, or a rasp bar drum, consisting of 6 beaters. The overall weight is 900kg. Capacity, based on average dry wheat, can reach 1000kg/h. The Minor is a larger thresher weighing 1400kg. Like the minorette it can be fitted with a rasp bar or a peg drum. Capacity can reach 2000kg/h. The minor thresher features a grain elevator consisting of a bucket and roller chain with single bagging-off chute. It is constructed from steel and mounted on a robust steel chassis.

ALVAN BLANCH DEV. CO. LTD.
Chelworth
Malmesbury, Wilts. SN16 9SG
U.K.

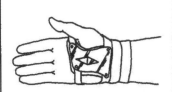

HUSKING HOOKS AND PINS

These husking hooks greatly speed the laborious task of removing the husk from corn cobs when this is carried out as a manual operation. When harvesting, too, is manual the husk is often left on the stem.

MAST HARNESS SHOP
Rt. 1, Box 228
Hazletown, Iowa 50641
U.S.A.

DUPLEX HAND-HELD MAIZE SHELLER

A simple, highly efficient hand-held sheller with the capacity to handle cobs of varying size. It is manufactured in cast iron for long life. Two sizes are available.

R. HUNT & CO. LTD.
Atlas Works, Earls Colne
Colchester, Essex CO6 2EP
U.K.

HAND CORN SHELLER AND SEED GRADER

This sheller ensures quick and easy shelling of corn. It is especially adapted for use in the selection of seed corn, as it does not break off the germ ends of the kernels.

DECKER MANUFACTURING COMPANY
312 Blondeau, Keokuk
Iowa 52632
U.S.A.

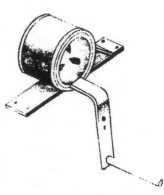

HAND-OPERATED MAIZE SHELLERS

The following firms manufacture a hand-operated maize sheller designed for bench mounting. Capacity may reach 500 cobs/h.

HAND-OPERATED SHELLER (illustrated)

ETS. A. GAUBERT
22 rue Gambetta
BP 24, 16700 Ruffec
FRANCE

MAIZE SHELLER NO. 994 Electrically moulded cast iron. Weight 4.5kg.

LANG FERRY & CIE
Brousseval (Hte-Marne)
52130 Wassy
FRANCE

SHELLER Cast iron body, steel crank with movable toothed disc on steel shaft with compression spring. Weight 6kg.

RENSON ET CIE
BP 23, 59550 Landrecies
FRANCE

MAIZE DECORTICATOR E 220 Spring assembly allows all sizes of corn cob to pass through. Weight 6kg.

S.E.C.A.
38260 La Cote St. André
FRANCE

AB/MSHB MAIZE SHELLER

This sheller is illustrated above. Cast iron stripper plate is spring loaded to accept cobs of any size.

ALVAN BLANCH DEV. CO. LTD.
Chelworth
Malmesbury, Wilts. SN16 9SG
U.K.

CHITETZE HAND-OPERATED MAIZE SHELLER

This sheller comprises two steel cylinders. The inner cylinder, fitted with two rows of internal teeth, is revolved within the outer by a hand crank. The sheller can be attached to any convenient wooden surface by nails or screws. The shellers are made in three sizes to suit the principle maize varieties grown in Malawi. The sizes relate to the circle formed by the ends of the teeth, and are 40mm, 33mm and 27mm respectively. The sheller has an output of 30kg/h of shelled maize from dehusked cobs.

PETROLEUM SERVICES (MALAWI) LTD.
Barnes Rd., Ginnery Corner
P.O. Box 1900, Blantyre
MALAWI

LILONGWE SHEET METAL LTD.
P.O. Box 47
Kanengo, Lilongwe 4
MALAWI

NDUME HAND-OPERATED MAIZE SHELLER

Constructed of three basic parts, of which two are strong and durable castings, the Ndume maize sheller is simple and robust. It can be mounted on a bench, table or post, and has a capacity of approximately 30kg/h of maize.

NDUME PRODUCTS LTD.
P.O. Box 62, Gilgil
KENYA

HAND-OPERATED MAIZE SHELLERS

ATLAS SHELLER Manufactured in the traditional design, this maize sheller (illustrated left) is constructed from cast iron for durability and long life. The Atlas maize sheller has a capacity of up to 120kg/h.

R. HUNT & CO. LTD.
Atlas Works, Earls Colne
Colchester, Essex CO6 2EP
U.K.

SMALL MAIZE SHELLER The small maize sheller (illustrated right) is designed so as not to break the eye of the corn seed, which is essential for germination. It has a capacity of 30-50kg/h of grain, and an overall weight of 20kg.

MOHAN SINGH HARBHAJAN SINGH
G.T. Road
Goraya 144 409 (Pb.) Distt.
Julundur (N.R.)
INDIA

HAND MAIZE SHELLERS

The following manufacturers all produce a spring maize sheller, with an average weight of 7kg.

They can be mounted on a stand, bench, box etc. and have an output of 30-100kg/h.

RAJAN UNIVERSAL EXPORTS (Mfrs.) PVT. LTD.
Post Bag 250, Madras 600 001
INDIA

CECOCO
P.O. Box 8
Ibaraki City, Osaka 567
JAPAN

DANDEKAR BROTHERS
Sangli-Shivaji Nagar, 416 416
Maharashtra
INDIA

IDEAL CASEMENTS (E.A.) LTD.
Box 45319, Nairobi
KENYA

COSSUL & CO. PVT. LTD.
123/367 Industrial Area
Fazalgunj, Kanpur, U.P.
INDIA

ALLIED TRADING COMPANY (INDIA)
Railway Road
Ambala City, Haryana
INDIA

CORN SHELLER

C.S. Bell produce this small corn sheller designed for dry ear maize and walnuts. It includes a cob ejector and tipping attachment. The spring adjusts to fit all size ears.

C.S. BELL CO.
170 W. Davis Street
Box 291, Tiffin, OH 44883
U.S.A.

MAIZE AND WALNUT SHELLER

A cast iron sheller weighing 10kg suitable for all types of large nuts, maize and corn.

CHAFF-CUTTERS (NZ) LTD.
P.O. Box 11, Ngatea
NEW ZEALAND

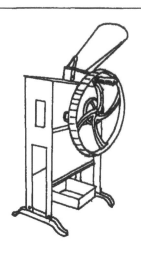

MAIZE SHELLERS

AB/MAH/3 MAIZE SHELLER This simple, hand-fed sheller (illustrated) has one hole to receive the cobs. It can be adapted for hand, pedal or power drive, the latter using a 0.5hp electric motor or petrol engine. Capacity, at 170rpm, is approx. 300kg/h. Overall weight is 86kg.

ALVAN BLANCH DEV. CO. LTD.
Chelworth
Malmesbury, Wilts. SN16 9SG
U.K.

MOTORIZED MAIZE SHELLER Powered by 0.5hp motor, this sheller has a capacity of 300kg/h, although it can be driven by hand. The overall weight is 66kg.

RENSON ET CIE
BP 23, 59550 Landrecies
FRANCE

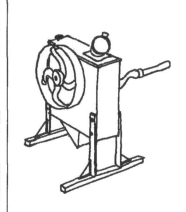

MAIZE SHELLERS

MAIZE SHELLER Hand- or motor-driven, with a capacity of 150-300kg/h (illustrated left).

SISMAR
B.P. 3214
20 rue Dr. Theze, Dakar
SENEGAL

HAND-OPERATED CORN SHELLER This machine can be operated by hand or by an electric motor.

UNION FORGINGS
Sherpur, Ludhiana, Punjab
INDIA

MAIZE HULLER NO. 3 M The 3 M (illustrated right) is hand-operated only, unlike the two models featured above. It can be regulated for different sizes of cob by means of a wing nut. Capacity is approx. 300-400kg/h.

ETS. CHAMPENOIS S.A.
Chamouilley, 52170 Chevillon
FRANCE

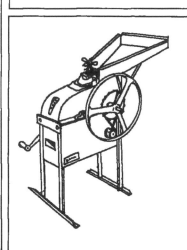

MAIZE SHELLERS

DM-2 CORN GRINDER This maize sheller (illustrated left) can be operated by hand or by a 0.25hp motor. It features a pressure lever regulated by a spring in order to adjust to various cob sizes, and a cleaning fan. Overall weight is 76kg.

PENAGOS HERMANOS & CIA. LTDA
Calle 28, No 20-80
Apartado Correos 689
Bucaramanga
COLOMBIA

HAND AND POWER MAIZE SHELLER A spring-type sheller (illustrated right) of all-steel construction with a cleaning fan. Power requirement is 1hp. Capacity ranges from 100-120kg/h (hand-operated) up to 200-300kg/h (power-operated). Overall weight is 70kg.

COSSUL & CO. PVT. LTD.
123/367 Industrial Area
Fazalgunj, Kanpur, U.P.
INDIA

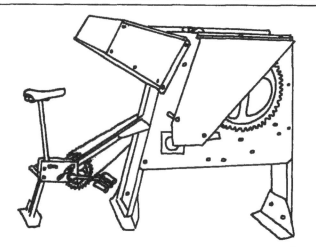

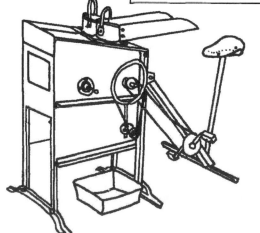

CYCLE MAIZE SHELLERS

Individual cobs are fed by hand into two holes and then drawn against revolving vertically mounted plate wheels.

AB/MSH/8 MAIZE SHELLER This model (illustrated above) has no sieving action, but a winnowing fan helps provide a clean sample. It can be powered by a petrol engine or ½hp electric motor (output 800kg/h).

ALVAN BLANCH DEV. CO. LTD.
Chelworth
Malmesbury, Wilts. SN 16 9SG
U.K.

COBMASTER MAIZE SHELLER This machine (illustrated right) can be hand- or pedal-operated or power driven (output up to 750kg/h).

R. HUNT & CO. LTD.
Atlas Works, Earls Colne
Colchester, Essex CO6 2EP
U.K.

2-HOLE SHELLERS

The illustration above shows the 2-hole sheller which will give two grades of maize. It has the following features:
● hand powered
● output of up to 10 bags per hour
● metal construction for durability
● grades into two grades
● adjustable for cob size
● lubricated roller bearings
● power pulley available

BAIN MANUFACTURING COMPANY (PVT.) LTD.
Box 1180, Harare
ZIMBABWE

JAMES NORTH & SONS LTD.
P.O. Box No. 3, Hyde
Cheshire SK14 1RL
U.K.

CORN HUSKER/SHELLER

CORN HUSKER SHELLER This machine is fitted with an axial flow motor capable of husking and shelling up to 600kg of maize per hour. It has a pneumatic box-winnowing system and is driven by a 2hp electric motor or engine. (Illustrated).

LAREDO MODELS S.A.
Industria E. Comercio
Rua 1 de Agosto
17.100 Bauru (SP)
BRAZIL

CORN SHELLER Two models are produced for husking, cleaning and sacking of any kind of corn. They can be powered by tractor, electric motor or petrol or diesel engine. Model SDMN -15/35 is the smaller machine with a power requirement of 5 to 8hp, and output of 900 to 2100kg/h.

NOGUEIRA IRMAOS SA
Rua XV de Novembro 781
P.O. Box 7
13970 — 1 Itapira, Sao Paulo
BRAZIL

SINGLE-EAR SHELLER

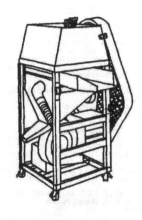

The single-ear corn sheller was developed primarily for use on test plots. It enables the operator to grade, count and size corn more efficiently. It is equipped with two 110 volt electric motors. One drives the shelling and separating operation and the other the blower for cleaning. The shaker pan has oval screen openings to allow all sizes of seed to be cleaned. The sheller is well constructed of tubular steel and 16 gauge sheet metal. It is mounted on rolling castors that can be locked when in position. It has belt and chain guards for safety. The height of the sheller is 125cm which makes observation of operating procedure possible at all times.

SWANSON MACHINE CO.
20-26 E. Columbia Avenue
Champaign, Illinois 61820
U.S.A.

MAIZE SHELLER M30

The M30 maize sheller standard model (illustrated) is supplied with a 240mm diameter pulley and carrier arms. The power requirement is 3 to 5hp and output is 2000 to 3000kg/h. The following accessories can be fitted:

- bagging elevator, outlet at 0.9m from ground
- bulk elevator, outlet at 1.9m from ground
- 3 point linkage with Glaenzer joint drive and protector to enable the sheller to be driven by tractor
- electric motor with a 120mm diameter flat pulley and belt
- lengthening port 1m in length to extend the bulk elevator or bagging elevator.

STE COMIA-FAO SA
27 bd. de Châteaubriant, BP 91
35500 Vitré
FRANCE

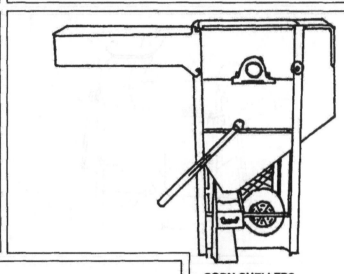

CORN SHELLERS

ALMACO EAR CORN SHELLER A self-cleaning unit with a rasp bar type shelling cylinder suitable for the grain breeder and similar research operations and is capable of single and multiple ear shelling. It requires a 2hp electric or 3hp petrol engine.

ALMACO
Box 296, 99 M. Avenue
Nevada, Iona 50201
U.S.A.

EDALTA 200 This corn sheller or steel construction can be powered by a 5 to 7hp petrol or diesel engine or a 3 or 4hp electric motor and produces up to 2100kg/h.

CIA PENHA MAQ. AGRÍCOLAS
Av. Brazil 1724, C.P. 477
Ribeirao preto
BRAZIL

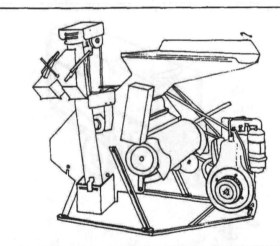

TROPICAL SHELLER

The Bamba tropical sheller is designed for African millet, sorghum and maize and can be operated by one person. It is powered by either a 5.5hp electric motor or 9hp petrol or diesel engine or with power take-off for any tractor. The output per hour is 1500kg of maize or 300-500kg of millet.

The grain can be collected in bags laid on the ground or the long auger can be attached for discharging directly into a trailer.

BOURGOIN S.A.
61 Av. Georges-Clemanceau
85110 Chantonnay, BP 17
FRANCE

MAIZE SHELLER

This machine (illustrated left) can either be hand-operated or power-operated, requiring a 5hp motor or engine. The shelling capacity is 1500kg/h.

DANDEKAR BROTHERS
(Engineers & Founders)
Sangli-Shivaji Nagar, 416 416
Maharashtra
INDIA

POWER MAIZE SHELLER

Dry cobs are fed into the shelling drum through a chute. Rotating iron beaters shell the grain (illustrated right). The power requirement is 3 to 5hp and output in 2000 to 2500kg/h

INTERNATIONAL MFG. CO (Regd.)
Hospital Road, Jagraon
Ludhiana, Punjab
INDIA

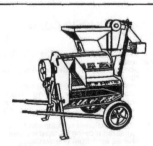

BAMBA CORN SHELLER

For millet, sorghum and maize, this machine requires an 8.5hp engine and has an hourly output of 300kg of millet or 1500kg of maize.

MARPEX
1 rue Thurot, 44000 Nantes
FRANCE

MAIZE SHELLERS

POWER-DRIVEN MAIZE SHELLER Operated with a 5hp electric motor, or with an oil engine (illustrated left). A winnowing fan is attached which separates the kernels from the cobs. The cobs are then expelled and the maize kernels are cleaned by the exhaust fan.

ALLIED TRADING COMPANY (INDIA)
Railway Road
Ambala City, Haryana
INDIA

MOHINDER MAIZE SHELLERS
Mohinder produce two power-driven maize shellers (illustrated right). The first has a power requirement of 3hp and an output of 10-15 quintals/h. The second, larger model has a power requirement of 5hp and a capacity of 18-20 quintals/h.

MOHINDER & CO. ALLIED INDUSTRIES
Kurali, Distt. Ropar, Punjab
INDIA

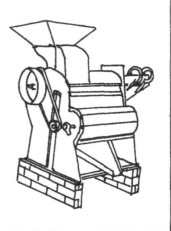

MAIZE SHELLERS

SPIKE-TOOTH MAIZE SHELLER This sheller features a blower for increased cleaning efficiency, and a lever to control the flow of grain. Two models are produced, the MS-10 and the MS-5, with power requirements of 10 and 15hp, and outputs of 15-25 and 10-15 quintals/h respectively. (Illustrated).

STANDARD AGRICULTURAL ENGINEERING CO.
824 & 825 Industrial Area B
Ludhiana A-141 003, Punjab
INDIA

AMUDA MAIZE SHELLER It can be powered by an electric motor or an oil engine. Again, two models are available, with power requirements of 3 and 5hp, and capacities of 1000-1200 and 1450-1650kg/h respectively.

RAJAN UNIVERSAL EXPORTS (MFRS.) PVT. LTD
Post Bag 250, Madras 600 001
INDIA

SHERPUR MAIZE SHELLERS

Both Union Forgings and Eicher produce the power-operated maize sheller illustrated above. It is manufactured from steel and can be operated with either an electric motor or a diesel engine. The power requirement is 5hp. Output ranges from 15-25 quintals/h of grain according to the rate of feeding. The overall weight of the Sherpur maize sheller is 200kg.

UNION FORGINGS
Focal Point
Sherpur, Ludhiana, Punjab
INDIA

EICHER GOODEARTH LTD.
Deepak 3rd Floor
13 Nehru Pl, New Delhi 110 019
INDIA

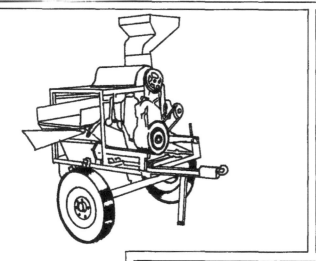

LAKAS KULIGLIG CORN SHELLER

The Lakas corn sheller has the following features:
- portable design, provided with tyres for simple mobility
- easy towing, towing-bar affixed.
- conical-shape shelling drum ensures high percentage (99-100 per cent) separation recovery and no broken grain.
- blower designed with air control for regulated blowing to separate clean shelled corn from fine waste.
- shaker separates shelled corn from cobs.
- labour requirement of 3, to feed shell and bag the grain.
- all steel construction.

P.I. FARM PRODUCTS
Km 16, Malanday
Valenzuela, Metro Manila
PHILIPPINES

AMAR MAIZE SHELLERS TYPE A AND TYPE B

This cylinder automatically separates the grain from the husks which are then expelled from the machine on three sides.
Technical specifications:

	Type A	Type B
power required (hp)	8	5
output of clean grain (quintals/h)	20-50	15-40
RPM	700	700
germination	98%	98%
height (m)	0.9	0.8

AMAR AGRICULTURAL IMPLEMENTS WORKS
Amar Street, Gill Road
Janta Nagar, Ludhiana-141003
INDIA

AB/MS/40 AND AB/MS/30 MAIZE SHELLERS

The AB/MS/40 sheller features a single shelling cylinder and a feed elevator. It has a power requirement of 10hp for electric motor or diesel/petrol engine drive. The capacity of the AB/MS/40 can reach 4 tonnes/h of shelled maize.

The AB/MS/30 (illustrated above) is a simplified model of the AB/MS/40 described above. It features the same single shelling drum unit, but has a feed chute instead of a cob elevator. The height of this feed chute is kept to a minimum by dispensing with a primary shaker shoe leaving the two sieve shoe to cope adequately with the reduced throughput. The AB/MS/30 is available as a static or mobile unit with a choice of drives by electric motor (power requirement 10hp) or diesel or petrol engine. Capacity is up to 3 tonnes/h of shelled maize.

ALVAN BLANCH DEV. CO. LTD.
Chelworth
Malmesbury, Wilts. SN16 9SG
U.K.

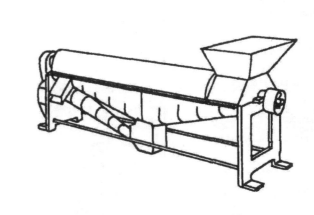

JYOTI GROUNDNUT THRESHER

The Jyoti groundnut thresher is an axial flow thresher, i.e. the plants move in a direction parallel to the beater axis. The pods are separated from the remainder of the plant in the threshing chamber so that the latter is expelled at the other end of the thresher. The pods, leaves and other impurities which remain then fall onto the sieve, where the leaves and light matter are removed by air from the blower. The clean pods then fall through the sieve and are discharged through the pod outlet. The thresher requires 10hp and is operated by 3-4 people. It can be used to thresh moist or dry groundnuts, and can also be adapted for other crops such as paddy, wheat and millet. Capacity ranges from 300-800kg/h of pods depending on the moisture content.

JYOTI LTD.
Bombay Shopping Centre
R.C. Dutt Road
Vadodara 390 005
INDIA

CECOCO PEANUT THRESHERS

This machine is designed to remove peanut pods from the haulm, chopping the remaining material into pieces of 10-12cm length. The power required is 1-3 or 2-4hp, depending on the model, and the capacity ranges from 250-370kg/h.

CECOCO
P.O. Box 8
Ibaraki City, Osaka 567
JAPAN

BEAN DEHUSKERS

LCS-300 BEAN SHELLER

LIM CHIENG SENG FACTORY
92-94 Sawanvithee Road
Nakom Sawan
THAILAND

CECOCO BEAN DEHUSKER (illustrated)

CECOCO
P.O. Box 8
Ibaraki City, Osaka 567
JAPAN

MOON MAIZE SHELLER

This maize sheller is designed for medium capacity. It comprises a cylindrical, peg-type drum. This design enables the drum configuration to be changed to suit differing crop conditions. The Moon maize sheller incorporates a primary cleaning fan. It has a power requirement of 4-8hp and can shell 2500kg of maize per hour.

R. HUNT & CO. LTD.
Atlas Works, Earls Colne
Colchester, Essex CO6 2EP
U.K.

WINNOWERS

HAND WINNOWER (illustrated below) A hand-operated winnower for cleaning jowar and other crops. Capacity is 100-150 bags/day. All-steel body fitted with bearing and pedestal.

MAHARASHTRA AGRO IND. DEV. CORPORATION LTD.
Rajan House, 3rd Floor
Near Century Bazar, Prabhadevi
Bombay 400 025
INDIA

RÖBER HAND WINNOWER (illustrated left) This is a hand-driven winnower featuring 3 sieves and a built-in ventilator. It has a capacity of 1.5 tonnes/h.

RÖBER GmbH
Friedrich-Wilhelm-Straße 79
4950 Minden (Westf 1), Postfach 1227
W. GERMANY

MINI WINNOWING MACHINE MEW-6 A hand-operated winnower constructed from sheet steel and angle iron.

MODERN ENGINEERING COMPANY
1A Anna Street, Velandi Palayam
Coimbator 641 025, Tamil Nadu
INDIA

WINNOWER 'JOLIE BRISE' Featuring 6 screens this winnower is designed for cleaning wheat, barley, rape seed, oats etc. It has a capacity of 1.5 tonnes/h and can be equipped either for hand or motor drive. The power requirement is 0.5hp. Overall weight is 130kg. Optional equipment available includes an elevator with sacking attachment, and extra upper screen, and an extra lower screen.

ASE EUROPE N.V.
Century Centre
de Keyserlei, 58 Box 1
B-2018 Antwerp
BELGIUM

CECOCO HAND WINNOWERS Cecoco produce two hand-operated winnowers. The first, the A1-model has a capacity of approximately 650kg/h, and an overall weight of 30kg.
The 'Hand grain winnower' is a smaller model weighing 17kg. Capacity is 650kg/h. A single-phase motor drive is available.
The hand grain winnower features three outlets (a) for whole grain or kernels, (b) for broken pieces, and immature grain and (c) for chaff, hulls and dust.

CECOCO
P.O. Box 8
Ibaraki City, Osaka 567
JAPAN

WINNOWING FANS

HAND WINNOWER This simple hand winnowing fan (illustrated above left) has a capacity of 500-800kg/h. Blade diameter is 120cm and overall weight is 25kg.

COSSUL & CO. PVT. LTD,
123/367 Industrial Area
Fazalgunj, Kanpur, U.P.
INDIA

WHEELBARROW-TYPE WINNOWING FAN Fixed to a stand with a single iron wheel at the front and two handles at the rear for easy mobility, this hand operated fan (illustrated above right) is driven by a series of bicycle chains and cogs. The stand is constructed from angle iron, and the blades have a diameter of 37cm. Sathiyawadi also produce a winnowing fan to be fitted to a hand tractor.

SATHIYAWADI STORES AND MOTOR TRANSPORTERS LTD.
P.O. Box 42, Kuronegala
SRI LANKA

CYCLE WINNOWER

This winnowing fan is fitted with a bicycle seat and pedal drive mechanism. The frame is all steel, and the blades have a span of 120cm. Capacity ranges from 1500-2000kg/h.

COSSUL & CO. PVT. LTD.
123/367 Industrial Area
Fazalgunj, Kanpur, U.P.
INDIA

BULLDOG TOOLS
Clarington Forge
Wigan
Lancashire WN1 3DD, UK.
Tel: (0942) 44281
Telex: 67325

BURGON & BALL LTD.
La Plata Works
Holme Lane
Sheffield S6 4JY, UK.
Tel: (0742) 338262
Telex: 54320 DOBPARK
Cable: SHOVELS WIGAN

CALDWELLS LTD.
Stockton Heath Forge
Dallam Lane
Warringhton, UK.
Tel: (0925) 36387
Telex: 627988
Cable: SHOVELS, STOCKTONHEATH
   WARRINGTON

COLUMBIAN CUTLERY CO. INC.
P.O. Box 123
440 Laurel Street
Reading
PA 19603-0123, USA.
Tel: (215) 374 5762/5894

EICHER GOODEARTH LTD.
Deepak 3rd Floor
13 Nehru Pl
New Delhi 110 019, India.
Tel: 681612
Telex: 031-4937 ETIL IN
Cable: TRACEICHER, NEW DELHI

FALCI
Via Cuneo 3/5/7
12025 Dronero (CN), Italy.
Tel: (0171) 918106/7/8
Telex: 21 24 51 FALCI I

**FERFOR (EMPRESSA INDUSTRIAL DE
   FERRAMENTOSE FORJACOS SARL)**
Apartado 16
4466 S Mamede de Infesta Codex, Portugal
Tel: 952066
Telex: 22262 FERFOR P
Cable: FERFOR

HERRAGUA
Herramientas Collings S.A. de Guatemala
Km. 27 Carretera al Pacifico
Apartado Postal 481-A
Amatitlan, Guatemala.
Tel: 0330 276/541
Cable: HERRAGUA

**HERRAMIENTAS AGRÍCOLAS
NACIONALES**
Panamericana sur Km.6 (San Bartolo)
Calle Catarama S/N
P.O. Box 2205, Ecuador.
Tel: 263300/610459
Cable: HANZA QUITO ECUADOR

HUTTON, T. & J., CO. LTD.
Phoenix Works
Sheffield S12 3XW, UK.
Tel: (0742) 485088
Telex: 547676

IMACASA
Finale Calle Liberatad Poniente
Parque Industrial Santa Lucia
Santa Ana, El Salvador.

JENKS & CATTELL LTD.
Phoenix Works
Neachells Lane Wednesfield
Wolverhampton WV11 3PU, UK.
Tel: (0902) 731271
Telex: 335647 JENCAT G

KENYA ENG. INDUSTRIES
P.O. Box 78052
Lokitaung Road
Off Likoni Road Ind. Area
Nairobi, Kenya.
Tel: 554180
Telex: 22866
Cable: LOCKS

KUMAON NURSERY
Ramnagar 244 715
Nainital U.P., India.
Tel: 39
Cable: NURSERY

KUMAR INDUSTRIES
Palghar District
Edathara 678 611
Kerala, India.
Tel: Parli 1
Cable: KUMAR EDATHARA

LYSBRO FABRIKER A/S
Postbus 219
8600 Silkeborg, Denmark.
Tel: 44506 824311
Telex: 63263 LYSBRO DK
Cable: LYSBRO

**MAHARASHTRA AGRO. IND. DEV
   CORPORATION LTD.**
Rajan House, 3rd Floor
Near Century Bazar
Prabhadevi
Bombay 400 025, India
Tel: 458211
Cable: KRUSHIUDYOG

MARTINDALE, RALPH, & CO. LTD.
Crocodile Works
Alma Street
Birmingham B19 2RR, UK.
Tel: 021-359 5611
Telex: 336872 RAMACO 5
Cable: CROCODILE, BIRMINGHAM

MODERN ENGINEERING COMPANY
1A Anna Street
Velandi Palayam
Coimbatore 641 025
Tamil Nadu, India.
Tel: 34765

**NORBERGS, SPAD &
   REDSKAPSFABRIKER, AB**
Vintergatan 7
591 32 Motala, Sweden.
Tel: (0141) 50065
Telex: 64904 SPADE S

SANDVIK AB
811 81 Sandviken, Sweden.
Tel: (14626) 260000
Telex: 47144 SANDVIKS
Cable: SANDVIK SANDVIKENSWED

SEYMOUR MAN. CO. INC.
P.O. Box 248
500 North Broadway
Seymour
IN 47274, USA.
Tel: (812) 522 2900
Telex: 276253-C of C SEYM

S.I.C.F.O.
66 à 78 av. Francois Arago
BP 205
92007 Nanterre Cedex, France.

SPALDING, A., & SON LTD.
Sadler Road
Lincoln LN6 3XJ, UK.
Tel: (0522) 691016
Telex: 56428

SPEAR & JACKSON (TOOLS) LTD.
St. Paul's Road
Wednesbury
W. Midlands WS10 9RA, UK.
Tel: 021-556 1255
Telex: 336549
Cable: SPEARTOOLS WEDNESBURY

**SYNDICAT DE L'OUTILLAGE AGRICOLE
ET HORTICOLE**
13 rue Beaujon
75008 Paris, France.
Tel: 227.02.76
Telex: 280900 FEDEMEC-SOAH

TRAMONTINA S.A.
Caixa Postal 1
95.185 Carlos Barbosa, (R.S.), Brazil.
Tel: (9054) 262-1400
Telex: 542371 TCFA BR
Cable: TRAMONTINA CARLOS BARBOZA
   RS BRAZIL

TROPIC
BP 706
Douala, Cameroon.
Tel: 42-42-56
Telex: TROPIC 5316 KN DOUALA
Cable: TLX TROPIC-DOUALA

TYZACK, W., SONS & TURNER, PLC
Little London Works
Sheffield S8 0UE, UK.
Tel: (0742) 51066
Telex: 54647 TYZTUR G

WOLF & BANGERT
Postfach 101047
Sieper Straße 41
5630 Remscheid 1, West Germany
Tel: (02191) 292048
Telex: 8513628 WOBA D
Cable: WOLFBANG

ZANA ZA KILIMO LTD.
P.O. Box 1186
Mbeya, Tanzania.
Tel: 2226
Telex: 51133
Cable: ZANAKILIMO

Printed in the USA
CPSIA information can be obtained
at www.ICGtesting.com
JSHW050200160824
68134JS00061B/2622